ADHD

RAISING AN EXPLOSIVE CHILD

THE STOP YELLING PARENTING
STRATEGIES TO DISCIPLINE EVEN THE
MOST UNRULY AND SCATTERED KID.

RACHEL ROSS

TABLE OF CONTENTS

DESCRIPTION

Harvey is an eight-year-old boy. Just like every little boy his age, Harvey loves to have fun by running around and playing. His mother, Rachel, has always taken pleasure in being a mother and watching Harvey grow into a sweet, adorable young boy. Suddenly, Harvey's behavior began to change for the worst; his hyperactiveness made it so he was not able to listen to his parents or focus on tasks, and he started having uncontrollable fits. Rachel wondered how she failed as a mother, because she could not understand what was wrong with her child and how she could help him. After evaluation from a psychologist, Harvey was diagnosed with ADHD. After Harvey's diagnosis, Rachel was able to dedicate her life to understanding her son's condition and how she could give him a better quality of life.

Parenting is a deeply rewarding part of life. It is a fulfilling experience that leaves many swollen with pride. The principles of parenting remain the same across the world; there may be small discrepancies here and there, but it is something innate in everyone. The most effective way to parent is to fulfill the needs of that specific child, because every child is different. On the other hand, parenting is infamously difficult, and it is accepted that there is no perfect formula to being a parent. In spite of this, expectant parents dream of a toothless gummy smile, ten perfect chubby toes, and ten perfect chubby fingers. The faultless physical form of a beautiful bouncing baby will throw the scent off from the irregularities that lie beneath the surface, which may take years to become noticeable.

With the randomness of genetics and illnesses, we have no way to predict exactly how our children will turn out. There are multitudes of things that could go wrong genetically. The things that can go wrong, however, should not discourage people from procreating. Rachel did not love Harvey any less after his diagnosis. Modern medicine ensures that all the different disorders, complexes, and conditions are diagnosed and treated earlier. Parents are no longer frustrated, wondering what is wrong with their child and if it can be fixed. Just like Rachel, parents of children who have ADHD can learn about the disorder and improve their parenting style to suit the needs of the child. In fact, Rachel quit her job so that she can provide this tailored information for all the parents who need it.

ADHD: Raising an Explosive Child: The Survival Guide for Kids with ADHD gives a new approach on how to be a positive parent who will empower children diagnosed with ADHD. The book not only assists in the theoretical aspect of raising a child with this disorder, but it also gives the reader strategies to help the child self-regulate. Be like Rachel, and give your child the chance to cope and thrive with everyday life by embracing their ADHD and learning to thrive through it.

INTRODUCTION

Rachel, The Professional and Family Woman

In today's world, women have more choices than staying home and bearing children. They can go out and conquer the corporate world, getting promotion after promotion until she is senior vice president or some other fancy title like that. Alternatively, she can choose to stay home and nurture her family. Women are more empowered than ever, and they are encouraged to chase their dreams more ferociously than ever before. In most cases, women juggle the two. Rachel is one such woman who decided to pursue her dreams and become a journalist. By working hard and staying focused on success, Rachel excelled at her job. At the same time, Rachel yearned to share that with someone. She felt as if she needed to start a family of her own, and share her life with a soul mate. Then she met Mike.

As if he innately knew what Rachel needed, Mike supported Rachel at home to ensure she thrived in her work life. Because Mike didn't stifle Rachel, their love grew deep and strong. They then decided to solidify their bond by getting married. Rachel was happy that she had found someone to share a life with, and she was also happy with her professional life. In spite of her professional success, there was still something missing. It seemed Rachel had it all, but she wanted more. She wanted to start a family. It wasn't because her biological clock was ticking, or any other external pressure that society imposes upon women. Deep within Rachel, she had a yearning to procreate with Mike and make a genetic copy of the both of them.

Mike, who was ever supportive, stood behind his wife as they began to try for a baby. They tried for a couple of months, and were successful in the third month. Rachel's pregnancy was easy, and she worked until her expected due date. At 32 years old, doctors had shown some concern, as Rachel was approaching the high risk pregnancy bracket of women over 35 years old. Good fortune was on their side as Rachel's pregnancy was healthy and uneventful. The day came for Rachel to give birth to her and Mike's first child, choosing to keep the gender a surprise until birth. As she heaved and pushed, Mike gave her constant assurance and encouragement. With one last big effort, Harvey was born.

Rachel took joy in watching Harvey grow. Although she enjoyed the pleasures of motherhood, she had not forgotten about her passion for journalism. Having Harvey meant that she had to accommodate her home life in her daily planning. Not only did she have to keep her professional life afloat, she had to juggle keeping Harvey fed, clean, and entertained. It was not easy having a professional job and raising a family with minimal help, but Rachel enjoyed it very much. There was nothing more satisfying than knowing she took care of her family and they took care of her. Every morning she woke up and every night she went to bed, a feeling of contentment would wash over Rachel; she knew she was where she was supposed to be, happy in her fairytale life with her Prince Charming and beautiful baby boy.

The Fairytale Ends

Unfortunately, things did not remain perfect for very long. There is a villain in every fairytale, and this one is no different. At some point in her life, Rachel would have to fight an evil force and conquer it, just like good conquers evil in every fairytale. The villain in Rachel's story is not as obvious as an old lady with a red apple or a conniving step mother, however. Rachel's nemesis came in a more stealthy manner, and she was grossly unprepared.

Every parent wishes their child a happy and carefree life unencumbered by diseases or disability, but that's not always how things go. As Harvey's fourth birthday rolled around, Rachel started noticing things about his behavior that worried her.

Harvey never missed an opportunity to shower Rachel with kisses and hugs, a characteristic she took pleasure in. She saw how sweet and adorable Harvey was, gentle-mannered and kind. Harvey reminded Rachel of Mike in a lot of ways. The issues became noticeable to Rachel when Harvey began associating more with his peers. It became apparent that Harvey would lose his focus very quickly and become distracted during play activities. Furthermore, Harvey would lash out if he couldn't get his way at home. He could not follow rules, he was extremely hyperactive and lively, and his communication style was not developed to the level of children his age. Rachel began to worry and think that something was wrong, but her friends and family reassured her that Harvey was young and would outgrow a lot of these issues.

Rachel consoled herself with the advice she was given by her loved ones. Even Mike thought that there was nothing seriously wrong with Harvey, and he too reassured Rachel not to worry too much about it, and that time would solve Harvey's behavior. It all culminated one December night as Rachel, Mike, and Harvey were spending time as a family. Harvey was his usual lively self, and he was ignoring reprimands from his parents to curb his excitement and liveliness. Rachel decided she was going to give Harvey an educational punishment. This reprimand set Harvey off in a way Rachel didn't expect, and he went into an explosive outburst. Rachel and Mike watched in horror as their son screamed, his face red with frustration, fists clenched and legs kicking. Harvey cried hysterically and Rachel tried her best to calm him down, but to no avail. Rachel felt helpless in that moment because she didn't know how to calm Harvey down, how to feel, or what had even gotten him so distraught. Eventually,

Rachel and Mike calmed Harvey down and put him to bed. That might, Rachel could not sleep.

As she replayed the evening's events in her mind, she could not help but wonder if Harvey's behavior was a cry for help. Rachel was pained wondering if she was doing enough to provide a conducive environment so her son can effectively communicate and express himself. A million questions raced through Rachel's mind: what was wrong with her son? Why was he behaving this way? Why was he having these hysterical outbursts? Paramount to all these questions was whether Rachel could help her son. She tossed and turned and tried to sleep, but she just couldn't. She had to do more to get her son the help he needed. Harvey's pain had become hers, and as a mother, Rachel knew she had to do something, anything to help her only son.

A New Beginning

Rachel called a psychologist friend of hers to chat about what has been happening recently with Harvey. The friend listened intently and suggested that Rachel bring Harvey in for an assessment, as she could not offer a diagnosis over the phone and without evaluation. The diagnosis came after an hour of evaluation in the psychologists office: Harvey had Attention-Deficit Hyperactivity Disorder (ADHD). Rachel had never heard of the disorder, so fear gripped her mind and her heart. Her ignorance made ADHD a villain that was bigger than it needed to be. After the initial shock, Rachel was glad she had an answer to what was wrong with her son, as the diagnosis gave them all an opportunity to find solutions. This was their chance to understand their son and how his mind worked.

The decision to quit her job came easily to Rachel, and she communicated it to Mike the day after Harvey's diagnosis.

Having a demanding full-time job would take away from the attention she needed to give her son with special needs. Rachel decided that she would have to dedicate her life to Harvey and his ADHD. The top priorities were to understand the disorder and how it affected a child, as well as how their family would have to adapt to a child with ADHD. Rachel was determined to focus on her son so that she was able to provide him with a better quality of life. She didn't know how she was going to do it, but she was determined to try.

It's been almost six years since Rachel quit being a journalist to care for Harvey full-time. After quitting her job as a journalist, she was able to throw herself into researching ADHD, and that became a passion that completely consumed Rachel. Not only has she come to understand ADHD as the least-known but most common disorder among children, Rachel has decided to share her knowledge and experience with others to further educate on the disorder, sharing the tools and strategies that she has used to cope and manage Harvey's ADHD.

This book is a testament to all those parents who are struggling to raise children with ADHD. Rachel took the passion to raise and understand her child and turned it into a career; she is a few exams away from becoming a child psychologist. With her knowledge and experience, Rachel would like to give the world a manual to help parents employ better tactics when communicating and raising children that have ADHD. This is a disorder that every parent can overcome so as to raise happy and healthy children that can be contributing members of society. A child with ADHD may feel lost, alone, or have difficulty managing their explosive outbursts, but this book will help minimize those feelings so they can be a child again, happy and free.

"This book is a gift from heaven, and I want to pass it down to every parent who ever felt as if they were failing their child, to

every parent who wondered what was wrong with their child when all that that child had was ADHD. I want you to know that I dedicated my life to this disorder so that I could understand my son, and with this book, you too can understand your child. You can overcome this disorder, you can provide specialized care for your child, and you can learn tools and strategies to be a good parent to a child with ADHD.

I never ever thought that something like this could happen to me in my life. I am a healthy person, and so is my husband. We eat a healthy and balanced diet and exercise regularly. I have no history of ADHD in my family, and neither does my husband. We could not have foreseen that our precious boy would have ADHD. It was shocking at first, but we had to process and recover from that shock in order to begin his healing process.

It is daunting to realize that you are the one in charge of the progress of his healing. I used to cry at night and ask Mike if I was doing the right thing, and he would reassure me that I am the best mother that Harvey could ask for. Even with all the support Mike gave me, we still had our disagreements from time to time over the course of treatment Harvey should have. Sometimes the disagreements were about finances because the diagnosis requires doctors, medications, and so many other different things. In the end, instead of tearing us apart, it brought us closer together.

We decided for ourselves and for Harvey that we were going to keep a positive and uplifting energy throughout this journey. We would challenge each other to find silver linings in the worst of scenarios, because that was the difference between succeeding and depression. Due to the fact that this is something that was new to us, failure was inevitable. We prepared ourselves to learn from every failure we faced. In the end, there were no failures and we only acquired lessons.

When you read this book, take it as a guide to follow, but remember that this journey is yours to take with your child. You have to explore your options and find out what works for you and your family. Keep an open mind throughout all of this, and remember that you are capable beyond measure. I went from being a journalist to being (well, almost) a child psychiatrist because I was so motivated to find answers for my son. You don't have to be a therapist to seek appropriate solutions for your child, but this book is a great start.

Should you ever feel alone, there is an entire online community of parents who are just where you are; scared and afraid of failing your child. What you felt has been felt a million times by a million other people, and just as they got through, you will get through too. Your child will thrive and achieve all they set out to achieve because you took the step to make their lives easier. Empowering a child to handle their disorder and disarm their symptoms is the best gift you can give as a parent. Special needs children can do as well for themselves as children with no disorders.

Take the time to commit to your family, your child, and conquering this disorder. It is not something that is easy to do, but with help and support, it can be done. I wish you luck during your journey to provide your child a better life. With the first step of purchasing this book, you have already shown your commitment to your child and I commend you. It is not easy, but here you are. I will walk with you and hold your hand through it all. These pages are your support system, and it is my purpose to make sure every parent faces ADHD with a heart filled with confidence and pride.

I'm ready to jump in. Are you?"

-Heartfelt hugs from Rachel, Mike, and Harvey.

CHAPTER 1

EXPLANATION OF ATTENTION-DEFICIT

HYPERACTIVITY DISORDER

In recent years, ADHD has become a common disorder that affects both children and adults. A study conducted in 2021 estimates that 5% of children across the world are affected by this disorder. The disorder can completely debilitate children and hinder their progress socially and mentally. When a parent looks around and sees their child's peers developing at an accelerated rate, they can wonder why their child is not developing at the same rate. Sometimes the child is behind, but sometimes there is something more nefarious going on in their mind.

ADHD is largely misunderstood, and the myths that surround the disorder can stigmatize those who have it. People do not understand what this developmental disorder is about, and the myths and stigma that surround it can cause a negative shift in the person who has it. This person may buy into the guilt and the shame that comes with the stigma. Unfortunately, these stigmas can cause those who have ADHD to attempt to take their own lives. For this reason, ADHD awareness is just as important as defining it or treating it.

In October 2021 (October being ADHD Awareness Month), the theme was 'Reframing ADHD: Discovering New Perspectives'. Short videos were posted addressing ADHD relationships, communication, treatment plans, ADHD parenting, and diagnosing children and adults, as well as co-occurring conditions. The initiative behind ADHD Awareness Month is to dispel myths and stigma about the disorder and share information about it so that people are not afraid of it, and to help those who have it not be ashamed anymore.

To begin the journey of education on what ADHD is, we have to delve into the scientific definitions and what characterizes the disorder. The scientific jargon has been simplified so that it is easy to understand and grasp, but it can get a little technical at times. Whatever is not easily understood can be discussed with the child's medical care provider so that the parents can understand better.

What is ADHD?

"The Diagnostic and Statistical Manual of Mental Disorders (DSM) provides the standard language by which clinicians, researchers, and public health officials in the United States communicate about mental disorders" (Regier et al., 2013). Published in May 2013, the current edition of the DSM is the fifth revision DSM-5. As the previous edition, and the first to mention ADHD, was the DSM-IV in 1994, this means that the definitions of ADHD in the DSM-5 are quite recent and carry more weight. It is important to note that mentions of hyperactive or attention-deficient children has been a topic in medicine over the past 200 years. ADHD has been a topic to be discussed for quite some time, but only recently has medicine made strides to hammer down on a more cohesive definition.

DSM-5 criteria for ADHD describes people with the disorder as those that "show a persistent pattern of inattention and/or hyperactivity–impulsivity that interferes with functioning or development" (Centers for Disease Control and Prevention, 2018). We will place our focus on ADHD in children up to 16 years old, and not on the definition of ADHD in adults.

Additional Conditions to be Met

In addition, the child must have had these inattentive or hyperactive-impulsive symptoms manifest before the age of 12 years old. The symptoms must be present in two more settings, such as at home and at school, or in front of friends or relatives. Further, there must be irrefutable evidence that these symptoms reduce the quality of or interfere with school, work, social or home functioning. Lastly, the symptoms should not occur during the course of another psychotic disorder or because of schizophrenia, and the symptoms should not be better explained by another mental disorder, such as mood, anxiety, dissociative, or personality disorder (Centers for Disease Control and Prevention, 2018).

As can be seen above, it is not easy to diagnose ADHD. A lot of conditions have to be met, as well as a specific combination of symptoms over a period of time, to be sure that it is indeed ADHD. Only after Rachel, Mike, and Harvey's teachers saw a combination of these symptoms over a certain period of time, during which it was clear they were interfering with his development, did they find it necessary to get some help. It was not an isolated event, either, as it was consistent, glaringly apparent, and disruptive. ADHD takes time to diagnose, but once the symptoms are present, they rarely go away or get better on their own.

What it Means to Have ADHD

Rachel could not have known why Harvey was behaving the way he was behaving or how he was feeling during his outbursts. It is not only important to understand what ADHD is, but also how a child is feeling during an outburst. Understanding the psychology of a child with ADHD assists parents or caregivers to understand what is going on in the child's mind, letting them equip themselves with tools to assist the child. Before Rachel could help Harvey, she had to understand him and where he was coming from.

Children are active beings that aren't good at receiving instructions; they play, fidget, and do not listen. For a child with ADHD, these normal shortcomings are amplified and intensified. These symptoms interfere with the child's normal development, and thus the child can experience feelings of frustration and get overwhelmed quite quickly. Children with ADHD are unable to regulate their emotions and struggle to plan, prioritize, pay attention, and remember details. It is not uncommon for children with ADHD to be labeled as the 'bad child' or the 'crazy child', and because of these negative terms, they may begin to feel this way about themselves (Low, 2021).

The effects of ADHD can make a child feel frustrated, confused, and disconnected. Children with ADHD can be less mature than their peers, which can lead to restlessness and feeling out of control. The child may feel inadequate due to the disruptions that ADHD is causing in their life. Once a parent can understand that the child is as frustrated as they are because they don't know what's going on, the healing can begin. Imagine being Harvey, feeling confused, overwhelmed, and not being able to regulate your emotions. Imagine being that scared little child who does not know what is going on with their own mind and body. Imagine being in such a terrible place and no one knows how to help you. It is a scary experience to be a child with ADHD.

Self-regulation is important for developing children, as it is the ability to understand one's own emotions and to manage them accordingly. This includes a person's behavior and reactions. Further, self-regulation assists children to develop adequate social skills and get along with one another. Self-regulation assists in controlling strong emotional reactions, being able to calm down after being very excited or very upset, helping to focus/re-focus on tasks, and controlling impulses.

Self-regulation is important because it allows the child to learn at school by enabling him to pay attention, sit still, and listen for the required amount of time in the classroom. By being able to control impulses, the child will be able to act in a socially acceptable way when in the company of peers. Your self-regulation also allows the child to make more friends, as they know how to behave in socially acceptable scenarios in such a way that makes them likable. If the child will be able to navigate new situations, they can become self-sufficient, independent, and need less of their parents' guidance.

Neurodevelopmental Disorders

"In DSM-5, NDDs are defined as a group of conditions with onset in the developmental period, inducing deficits that produce impairments of functioning. NDDs comprise intellectual disability (ID); Communication Disorders; Autism Spectrum Disorder (ASD); Attention-Deficit/Hyperactivity Disorder (ADHD); Neurodevelopmental Motor Disorders, including Tic Disorders; and Specific Learning Disorders" (Morris-Rosendahl, 2020).

Simply put, neurodevelopmental disorders are those that affect the functionality of the brain. Depending on the severity of the disorder, a person can either live a relatively normal life, or they may require special care for the duration of their lives. Common neurodevelopmental disorders include schizophrenia, ADHD, autism, and Tourette's syndrome. ADHD is a neurodevelopmental disorder, meaning that the brain function of the affected child is impaired. This is why the child is unable to regulate their emotions and prevent outbursts, as the dysfunction that happens in the brain makes it hard for the child to self-regulate. For example, a neurodevelopmental disorder prevents the child from being able to apply long periods of mental effort or following instructions.

Hyperactive Children

Hyperactivity, as a medical term, is defined as chronic sustained excessive motor activity, which is a cause for complaint both at home and at school ("Hyperactive Children," 1973). The APA Dictionary of Psychology (n.d.) defines hyperactivity as a condition wherein the sufferer experiences spontaneous gross motor activity or restlessness that is excessive for the age of the individual. Children are generally very active beings compared to adults. They are excitable, and so they tend to enjoy being on the go and never quite keeping still. Therefore, it is necessary to distinguish between a lively child and one that is hyperactive. The word hyperactive is often misused, which creates confusion on what hyperactivity means in children and the significance of calling or diagnosing a child as hyperactive. A child who is lively is far from being hyperactive, because hyperactivity comes with a cluster of symptoms that negatively affect the child's life.

Hyperactive children are often referred to as those with ADD, ADHD, or hyperkinetic disorder. The terms are often interchangeable, as they can all describe a child who is hyperactive. A lively child who is full of energy is a common occurrence, and a lot of children are like that. Hyperactive children, on the other hand, are described as those that experience a combination of the following symptoms: short attention span and poor powers of concentration, impulsiveness, irritability, explosiveness, variability, and poor school work (Laufer & Denhoff, 1957).

The liveliness of a child only becomes a concern when it interferes with the development of the child. For example, if the child cannot complete a task that they are assigned because they have a short attention span or can't apply prolonged efforts of concentration, this will negatively affect their school work and prospects of success. This on its own does not mean the child is hyperactive. If it is also combined with the child talking excessively, fidgeting, climbing, and not being able to keep seating for appropriate stretches of time, interrupting others, and the child being unable to play quietly, then maybe the child may be diagnosed as hyperactive.

Inattentive Children

When the world hears ADHD, they automatically think of the hyper child who is fidgety and has extreme outbursts. We cannot speak about the hyperactive child without also exploring the inattentive child, because they are different sides of the same coin. The child with ADHD due to inattention is not as disruptive as the hyperactive child, but their symptoms can cause the same type of frustration and confusion. It is also important to distinguish between a child who is inattentive and one who has ADHD due to inattention. The APA Dictionary of Psychology (n.d.) defines inattention as a state in which there is a lack of concentrated or focused attention, or where the attention drifts back and forth.

It is not a strange thing to observe that children often get bored easily, and that they may have a limited attention span. This natural occurrence of how children behave makes it easier for the term inattentive to be used, but this does not mean that they have ADHD. It becomes ADHD when there are more than six symptoms present for over six months. The symptoms must have a negative effect on the child's development at school and at home. This means that before a child is diagnosed with ADHD due to inattention, all other potential causes have to be ruled out first.

A child who has ADHD due to inattention will often miss details and become distracted easily. They are more prone to becoming bored easily, and having difficulty focusing on the task at hand. Children with ADHD due to inattention will struggle to organize new information, have difficulty learning, and following instructions, as well as getting confused easily. They process information slower than others and struggle to follow instructions. However, these cannot be the sole symptom, as the child has to display at least six to be diagnosed with ADHD. The symptoms of inattention should drastically lower their ability to learn and develop at the same pace as their peers.

Takeaways

This chapter has explained what ADHD is, as well as giving an overview of what it means to have the disorder. It is tough to exist as a child who has yet to learn how to understand themselves or to articulate the spectrum of emotions human beings feel. It is even worse when your brain is incapable of regulating that spectrum of emotions. ADHD in children is not their burden to carry alone, but rather something that they have to experience with their family, as well as their educators.

There is a popular saying 'it takes a village', and that applies here when you look at what is needed for the upbringing of a child who has ADHD. To diagnose a child of this disorder, it is not just the parents' word that has to be considered, but also the word of other adults who are in contact with this child consistently outside of the home. The disorder is frustrating and depressing to experience, but we still have to understand it thoroughly before we can attempt to assist those who are affected by it.

CHAPTER 2

IDENTIKIT OF ADHD - SYMPTOMS,

CHARACTERISTICS AND BEHAVIORS

As with any disorder, the earlier the signs are noticed, the sooner the child will get help. It was not a good feeling for Rachel to feel like she failed Harvey. Parenting is difficult on its own without mothers and fathers having to feel inadequate. It is a bumpy road, but all parents want to do their best. Rachel felt as if she could not help Harvey, and the idea that she could not take away her son's pain hurt her. Only after Rachel equipped herself with knowledge of the signs was she able to take Harvey to a psychologist to get checked.

If a parent knows when, why, and how a disorder begins, they are more likely to recognize the signs and do something about it before they adversely affect the child's life. Adjusting to a child with ADHD when they are younger is easier to adapt to, but recognizing it at teenagehood may require more effort from parents to change their parenting styles to meet the needs of their teenager who has ADHD. In spite of this, it is never too late to reorganize the signs and get a child with ADHD the help they need.

When Does ADHD Begin?

Some people wonder when ADHD actually begins. Does it begin after a certain age? Is it caused by continued exposure to various things? A lot can be said about the theories surrounding when ADHD begins, but we can rely on what is stated in the Diagnostic and Statistical Manual for Mental Disorders. In DSM-IV, it was outlined that symptoms in a child suspected to have ADHD must have been present in said child before the age of 7. This was the criterion used before the changes made in DSM-5, which drastically impacted how ADHD was viewed and how symptoms first began to be understood further. ADHD was classified as a neurodevelopmental disorder to highlight that there is correlation between ADHD and brain development, as well reflect the decision by DSM-5 to eliminate the DSM-IV chapter that includes diagnoses made in infancy, childhood, or adolescence. The more psychologists understand ADHD, the more they understand that the beginning of the disorder is not black and white. It's not as simple as saying it begins in preschool or during infancy, because ADHD can develop later for adults than children.

Changes in criteria for ADHD were made in order to improve detention of the disorder in adults. The DSM-5 states that the onset criterion is several inattentive or hyperactive-impulsive symptoms that are present prior to age 12 (Substance Abuse and Mental Health Services Administration, 2016). Diagnosing hyperactivity began in the 1970s with psychologists observing these symptoms in children. This then saw psychology recognizing hyperactivity in adults in the 1990s, which led to adults being diagnosed with ADHD. DSM-5 puts the age at 12 to not only analyze when ADHD begins for children, but also when it begins for adults. There is no definitive answer of when ADHD begins in children, but the DSM-5 offers a criterion of symptoms manifesting before 12 years old. Sometimes, symptoms can even start as early as three years old. For Rachel, it seems the symptoms came early for Harvey at four years old. Every child is different and is exposed to different environments, so the manifestation of ADHD will happen at different times. Symptoms of ADHD that manifest in a child at ten years old are no less significant than symptoms that manifest at four years old; the key is to recognize them when they do.

Why Parents Underestimate or Ignore the Symptoms of ADHD

Parents often romanticize their journey as a parent, meaning they can be in denial about their child's disabilities or disorders. This is because everyone sees their child as perfect, and even if the child is not perfect, no parent wants to admit that. It is absolutely heartbreaking for a parent to realize that their child has a disorder. This is often met with the parent sticking their head in the sand and hoping it will go away, but ADHD rarely does. Situations like these are even worse in more conservative societies, where seeking medical attention from a physiologist is frowned upon. A parent can be seen as a failure if they are unable to rectify their child's shortcomings on their own. For this reason, symptoms of ADHD can go ignored.

It is a common perception that children are lovely and hyperactive; they don't listen and they don't follow instructions on tasks. Even when Rachel worried that something was wrong with Harvey, her loved ones assisted her that this was a stage all children went through. But to what end? Had Rachel not acted on her intuition, Harvey may have not gotten the help he so desperately needed. Parents need to be able to differentiate when children are being lively in the normal course of childhood and when children are being hyperactive due to ADHD. The former is usually harmless and does not interfere with the child's progression at school and in life, whereas the latter is clearly disruptive to the child's development.

Resistance from family is expected, but feedback from teachers at the child's school could corroborate what is happening at home. Children misbehave at home because they can get away with it, while at school, a child can be a completely different person. The home is also a place of leisure and comfort, meaning that a child may feel more of an opportunity to let loose emotionally. If the child is still exhibiting symptoms of ADHD at school, a parent can use that to corroborate the behavior they witness at home. Parents are socialized to think there is nothing wrong with a hyperactive or inattentive child, and that makes it harder to recognize the symptoms of ADHD.

Parents are disciplinarians. They try to correct behavior and mold the child into the best human they can be. Parents want nothing more than for their child to be an upstanding member of society. This means that when the hyperactive or inattentive behavior begins, the parent can blame other things instead of facing the issue at hand. For example, the liveliness of a child may be blamed on their diet or their refusal to eat vegetables. Some people blame technology for a child being unable to focus. Some have even gone so far as to blame hyperactive behavior on how parents raise their child, more specifically in how they spoil them. Some parents just chalk ADHD symptoms up to bad behavior and leave it at that.

The kind of culture that the child is growing up in will determine whether or not parents take ADHD symptoms seriously or not. In cultures that are more conservative, the parents are more concerned about what people will say about their child than facing the issue at hand. These types of societies value how the family appears to the outside world, rather than developing genuinely healthy connections within their families. A culture like this is detrimental to the child's prospects, and there is a low chance that the parents will admit that the child has a disorder and needs help.

Parents who have the financial means to support their family and whatever ailments they come with are more willing to accept that a child may have some type of disorder. When a family's socio-economic status is not one that can accommodate a disorder that may cost them financially, they may feel the urge to sweep certain noticeable symptoms under the rug. Healthcare is a large expense in every household across the world, and some families cannot afford to properly treat a child who has ADHD without breaking the bank. If a child is symptomatic in these families, then their parents are more likely to downplay their symptoms.

All these reasons are why parents deflect or ignore the ADHD symptoms when they first start to present themselves in their child. Sometimes ADHD symptoms are ignored due to a parent's fear and insecurity, and some parents do not know if they have what it takes to raise a child with ADHD. However, ignoring them won't make them go away. Ignorance can be a driving factor of ignoring a child's symptoms. The only downfall here is that the child will suffer and their quality of life will be drastically reduced.

Learning to Recognize the Early Signs of ADHD

It may be difficult to recognize the signs of ADHD because the early symptoms are what is considered normal in a child. Furthermore, ADHD evaluations happen mostly when the child is at an age where they can attend school, meaning earlier periods may be ignored. Even though the behavior a child exhibits may be considered normal for their age, it is still important for a parent to take note and mention it to the child's pediatrician. Keeping medical professionals in the loop about your suspicions and worries may be the difference between a happy ADHD-diagnosed child and an undiagnosed, disgruntled child. Even if family and friends can view a parent as paranoid for thinking their child has ADHD, they still should know what to look out for.

Difficulty Focusing or Concentrating

Is the child able to sit through a brief bedtime story? Is the child able to start and complete an age-appropriate puzzle without interruption? If this is a behavior that is consistent regardless of who is supervising the child, then it may be something to pay attention to.

Difficulty Listening

When the child is spoken to, are they able to hold the conversation to completion? Does the child stay on topic, or does the child ask about things that are unrelated to the conversation? Inability to listen is an early sign of ADHD.

Unable to Regulate Behavior

Is the child able to regulate their emotions? Does the child have intense explosive reactions? Is the child able to regulate when they're feeling excited, happy, sad, or frustrated? When it appears that the child is having a meltdown at every turn, then this becomes a symptom to keep an eye on as an early symptom of ADHD.

Extreme Hyperactivity

Lively children are a normal occurrence, but when a child is only able to keep still in their sleep, it may be a cause for concern. Is the child in constant motion and continually fidgeting? Are they able to keep still at all? Being excessively hyperactive may be an early indicator of ADHD.

Negative Impacts of ADHD in a Child's Life

Imagine having a family that functions wonderfully aside from one family member. Imagine everyone knowing what they're supposed to do except this one. The child is a good child who shows love and affection to their family members, but for some reason, the child sometimes can't do as they're told. The child is unable to sit still for long enough to complete their homework or clean their room. No matter how many times the child is sent to the naughty corner or has their privileges revoked, they just cannot seem to tow the line.

Harvey was that child, and Rachel and Mike could not understand why they couldn't reach him. Sometimes, if things got really bad, Harvey would spiral into an uncontrollable fits of anger where he became inconsolable, and his parents would be unable to calm his extreme reactions to their discipline measures. The lack of peace and the intense disruption that comes with the consequences of the symptoms of ADHD can create friction in any household. The child is not in control of their behavior and will push the limits of tolerance in their parents, siblings, and other family members. This may make immediate family members resent the child, even though this disorder is not their fault.

If the household that a child is growing up in is a two-parent household, dealing with ADHD can lead to relationship problems. It is easier to agree on parenting styles for children that don't have any kind of disorder, but when it comes to dealing with ADHD, conflict may arise surrounding the course of action that they need to take. One parent may accept that their child needs to be put on medication to alleviate symptoms, but the other parent may be against that, especially if they feel like the child is too young to be put on medication. These kinds of conflicts can lead to depression in one or both parents, and can ultimately cause the separation of the parents. The breakdown of the nuclear family will adversely affect the child.

The school system may not be equipped to serve the needs of all children, but it is required by law in most countries that children attend school. Unfortunately, children with ADHD are at a disadvantage in a regular classroom. A child with ADHD may not be able to concentrate for long periods of time, meaning they may not be able to listen, pay attention, or be able to regulate their behavior and emotions during class time. The classroom setting is not conducive for learning if the child has ADHD, meaning the child can be at a higher risk of dropping out, expulsion, and poor academic performance. They will struggle to keep up with their peers in the classroom who don't have ADHD.

As soon as a child is put into a school, they are also placed in a social situation where they have to interact with their teachers as well as their peers. Children with ADHD may struggle with both peer and family relations (Peasgood et al., 2016). They are at higher risk of bullying others and of being bullied; conduct issues can arise and antisocial behaviors can develop. A child with ADHD may get involved in fighting, as well as early substance experimentation.

Emotionally, ADHD can disorient a child because it prevents them from being able to regulate their emotions. A child diagnosed with ADHD may suffer from anxiety, low self-esteem, and poor psychosocial health, and they will experience a subpar quality of life because of this. These implications of ADHD also affect the child's siblings and family. The siblings may resent the child with ADHD for having all their parents' attention, or they may develop a responsibility to be the child's caretaker. Living with a child who has ADHD can cause there to be constant disruption of family life, which can be chaotic and exhausting to the sibling (Peasgood et al., 2016).

Presentations of ADHD

Based on the various types of symptoms that can occur, there are three different presentations of ADHD. The first presentation of ADHD is the predominantly inattentive presentation, where there are mostly symptoms of inattention but not those of the hyperactivity-impulsivity kind over a period of six months.

The second presentation of ADHD is the predominantly hyperactive-impulsive presentation, in which the opposite is true. Here, there are symptoms of hyperactivity-impulsivity and not inattention present in the child for a period of six months. Lastly, the third presentation of ADHD is a combined presentation, where symptoms of both inattention and hyperactivity-impulsivity are present over a period of six months. It is important to note that symptoms can change over time, meaning a child's presentation can also change. A child considered to have a combined ADHD presentation can move toward an inattention presentation or a hyperactive-impulsive presentation, or vice versa.

To understand the various presentations of ADHD, we need to understand the various aspects of the symptoms as given by the DSM-5. They will be broken up into two main sub-categories: inattention, and hyperactivity and impulsivity.

Inattentive Presentation of ADHD

For a child up to the age of 16 to be diagnosed with ADHD due to inattention, they need to display six or more of the following symptoms, for at least six months, that are inappropriate for their developmental level:

- The child fails to give detailed attention to school work, or makes careless mistakes in school work or other activities.

- The child often fails at devoting basically their attention on given tasks or play activities.

- The child does not seem to listen when they are directly spoken to.

- The child is unable to follow through on school work, chores, or duties in the workplace, becoming sidetracked or losing focus easily.

- The child has trouble organizing tasks and activities.

- The child avoids or dislikes tasks that require prolonged mental effort, such as homework or schoolwork.

- The child often loses things required for tasks, such as eye glasses, stationary, keys, books, mobile phone, etc.

- The child is often easily distracted.

- The child is often forgetful in daily life. (Centers for Disease Control and Prevention, 2018).

Hyperactive-impulsive Presentation of ADHD

For a child up to the age of 16 to be diagnosed with ADHD due to hyperactivity or impulsivity, they need to display six or more of the following symptoms, for at least six months, that are inappropriate for their developmental level:

- The child often fidgets, squirms, cannot sit still, or taps their hands or feet.

- The child leaves their seat when they are expected to remain seated.

- The child runs around or climbs when it is inappropriate to do so.

- The child cannot partake in leisure or play activities quietly.

- The child is often on the go as if driven by a motor.

- The child talks excessively.

- The child blurts out answers to a question that has not yet been completed.

- The child is unable to or has difficulty waiting their turn.

- The child often interrupts others or intrudes on others, such as during games or interrupting others during conversations (Centers for Disease Control and Prevention, 2018).

Combined Presentation of ADHD

Sometimes, a child's symptoms can fall in both the above mentioned categories, having both some hyperactive symptoms and some inattentive symptoms. If both are present in the child for a period over six months, then the child may be diagnosed with the combined presentation of ADHD. To recognize these symptoms in a child, a parent will need to know the symptoms of a hyperactive-impulsive presentation, as well as the symptoms of an inattentive presentation.

CHAPTER 3

DIAGNOSIS AND CAUSES

A diagnosis, as described by the APA (n.d.), is the process of figuring out the nature of disease or disorder based on symptoms via tests and other evidence. Diagnoses are not made by regular people on the street, and Rachel on her own could not diagnose Harvey of ADHD. Yes, he exhibited some symptoms, but she did not have the authority to definitely decide what disorder Harvey had. There are people trained to provide such information and assist in providing those diagnoses. For a condition such as ADHD, it would not be a regular doctor, but a doctor trained to identify neurodevelopmental disorders.

Parents can first begin with the child's general practitioner (GP) or their pediatrician. There's no need to worry about where to find a doctor who will assess a child for ADHD, because GPs and pediatricians have all the information necessary to make an adequate assessment. They know how to discern between a lively child and one that is showing signs of ADHD, and they have the knowledge of when a child should be further assessed by a specialist. There are systems in place in the medical profession that ensure that no child is left undiagnosed or without help when they need it.

There is controversy surrounding diagnosing ADHD, as there are people who question if ADHD is a bona fide diagnosis or some kind of scam or fraud concocted by the medical profession. Renowned Harvard psychologist Jerome Kagan is one of ADHD's biggest critics. Keegan strongly doubted that ADHD existed to begin with, and that it had a weak neurological basis. Furthermore, Kagan thought it was a disorder invented by the big pharmaceutical companies in order to defraud the public and pump money out of them via the endless prescriptions they'll be writing out.

Alongside the diagnosis, there is a concern over medication of ADHD, and the numbers are rising and more and more children are being diagnosed and medicated. Is ADHD simply a social construct that has no basis in biology, or is it a serious illness that can present dire life consequences for an individual if left untreated? Whether or not ADHD is shrouded in controversy, children are still suffering and need to be diagnosed in order to seek help. Can we risk leaving people undiagnosed to feed into the narrative that ADHD is made up? There is enough scientific evidence that proves that ADHD is not a fraud and is a legitimate concern globally.

The prevalence of ADHD is higher in countries that have higher income, with research showing that to male children have double the chance of being diagnosed with ADHD than female children. Severe ADHD is largely diagnosed at four years old, while moderate ADHD is diagnosed around six years old. For mild cases of ADHD, seven years old is the average age of diagnosis. ADHD is not something that's easy to understand, meaning it must be left to the professionals to break down to the layman.

Who can Diagnose ADHD?

Psychiatrists

A psychiatrist is a physician whose specialty is in diagnosing, treating, preventing, and studying mental, behavioral and personality disorders (APA Dictionary of Psychology, n.d.). A psychiatrist goes through a training period of around 14 years before they are fit to practice; they partake in psychiatric residency for four years, interning in a hospital then moving onto learning diagnosis and treatments including medication. This thorough training makes a psychiatrist competent to diagnose and treat ADHD.

Pediatricians

A pediatrician is a physician who specializes in the care and treatment of disease in infants, children, and adolescents. This care can include neurodevelopmental disorders such as ADHD. Pediatricians see numerous disorders in their patients over their careers, which is why they have the capacity to diagnose ADHD. A pediatrician's medical training may span over a decade long; they train as a general practitioner for around eight years, alongside an added three years in pediatric residency. From there, they can further specialize into numerous different fields, such as neonatology, rheumatology, nephrology, and many more.

Neurologists

Neurology deals with the nervous system in the human body. This branch of medicine is concerned with the nervous system in its healthy state, as well as in its diseased state (APA Dictionary of Psychology, n.d.-b). A neurologist diagnoses and treats patients who have suffered from a stroke, dementia, headaches, and other disorders. Neurology is directly related to neurodevelopmental disorders, which is why this medical practitioner would be equipped to assess a child who has ADHD symptoms.

Psychologists

According to the APA Dictionary of Psychology (n.d.-c), a psychologist is "an individual who is professionally trained in one or more branches or subfields of psychology." The study of mind and behavior is what we know as psychology. Just as mentioned above with other medical physicians, a psychologist undertakes almost a decade or more of medical training. Psychologists can work in various places, including schools, hospitals, laboratories, prisons, or private practice. ADHD affects the mind of the affected child as well as their behavior, which makes this medical practitioner a suitable authority to assess a child with ADHD symptoms and possibly offer treatment.

ADHD Assessment

A parent will always have a suspicion that something may be wrong with their child. Sometimes the suspicion is a phase or paranoia, but other times the suspicion is spot on and turns out to be ADHD. Like Rachel, the important thing is to get treatment for the child. She took Harvey directly to a psychologist because her friend is one. Not everyone is that fortunate, but we all have access to general practitioners. They make the initial assessment and then refer to any of the above mentioned doctors, who will then offer a diagnosis after assessment.

Before we can get to the assessment, the parent of the child needs to prepare certain information for the child's appointment. The parents should have a complete list of any symptoms or difficulties the child is displaying at home or at school. This means the parent should liaise with the child's teachers to ensure they have the full picture of the child's behavior. The parent should note key stressors in the child's life, as well as any recent life changes, like starting a new school, a divorce, or moving homes. Medications being taken should be mentioned as well as if the child has been previously tested. School report cards should be provided to the professional for them to see if the child is thriving at school or not. Lastly, the parent should come prepared with any questions they may want to ask.

The child's symptoms could be caused by any number of other disorders, so parents should be prepared for that and expect anything. Numerous disorders or medical conditions resemble ADHD, such as learning or language disorders, mood disorders, vision or hearing impairments, autism spectrum disorder, sleep disorders, and brain injuries. There are certain questions that the medical practitioner will ask to ascertain if indeed the child has ADHD. There is no specific test for the disorder, but it is a series of questions that the parent is asked.

"The diagnosis of ADHD requires a comprehensive clinical assessment including a detailed patient history, clinical interview and observation, and a thorough physical examination. Ideally, the process requires several visits if done thoroughly; if limited to one visit, physicians should allot at least one hour to perform the initial assessment" (Adesman, 2001).

The parents' interview is a critical part of the interview, as the child can behave differently whilst in the physician's office. The following questions will be asked according to the DSM-5 prerequisites of which symptoms should be present for ADHD. The parent must answer if the symptom happens not at all, just a little, often, or very often:

For inattention

1. Fails to give attention to details or makes careless mistakes in school work, work,   or during other activities (e.g., overlooks or misses details, work is inaccurate).

2. Has difficulty sustaining attention to tasks or play activities (e.g., has difficulty remaining focused during lectures, conversations, or lengthy reading).

3. Does not seem to listen when spoken to directly (e.g., mind seems elsewhere, even in the absence of any obvious distraction).

4. Does not follow through on instructions and fails to finish schoolwork, chores, or duties in the workplace (e.g., starts tasks but quickly loses focus and is easily sidetracked).

5. Has difficulty organizing tasks and activities (e.g., difficulty managing sequential tasks, difficulty keeping materials and belongings in order, messy, disorganized with work, has poor time management, fails to meet deadlines).

6. Avoids, dislikes, or is reluctant to engage in tasks that require sustained mental effort (e.g., schoolwork or homework, preparing reports, completing forms, reviewing lengthy papers).

7. Loses things necessary for tasks or activities (e.g., school materials, pencils, books, tools, wallets, keys, paperwork, eyeglasses, mobile telephone).

8. Is easily distracted by extraneous stimuli (for older adolescents, may include unrelated thoughts).

9. Is forgetful in daily activities (e.g., doing chores, returning calls, keeping appointments).

For hyperactivity:

10. Fidgets with or taps hands or feet or squirms in their seat.

11. Leaves seat in situations in which it is inappropriate (in adolescents or adults, may be limited to feelings of restlessness).

12. Unable to play or engage in leisure activities quietly.

13. Has difficulty playing or engaging in leisure activities quietly.

14. Is "on the go" or acts as if "driven by a motor" (e.g., is unable to be or uncomfortable being still for extended time in situations like restaurants or meetings, may be experienced by others as being restless or difficult to keep up with).

15. Talks excessively.

For impulsivity:

16. Blurts out an answer before a question has been completed (e.g., completes people's sentences, cannot wait for a turn in conversation).

17. Has difficulty waiting his or her turn (e.g., while waiting in line).

18. Interrupts or intrudes on others (e.g., butts into conversations, games, or activities, may start using other people's things without asking or receiving permission. For adolescents and adults, may intrude into or take over

what others are doing) (DSM-5 ADHD SYMPTOM CHECKLIST, n.d.).

The parent will answer when they first start noticing behaviors that occur often and very often, if the symptoms affect the child's functioning in two or more settings, and if the symptoms occur at home, at school, or socially. There are also various optional scales that can be used, such as the parent-completed Child Behavior Checklist, the Teacher Report Form (TRF) of the Child Behavior Checklist, the Conners' Parent and Teacher Rating Scales (the long form), the ADD-H Comprehensive Teacher Rating Scale (ACTeRS), and the Barkley Home Situations Questionnaire and School Situations Questionnaire (Adesman, 2001).

Executive functions tests will also be done on the child to determine the child's ability to manage tasks at home and at school. The tests evaluate higher order cognitive abilities, which are associated with the frontal lobe of the brain. Executive functions include problem solving skills (reasoning, planning, and organization) and flexibility in thinking, as well as the ability to digest and integrate feedback from others. After physically assessing the child and their symptoms, the doctor will be able to see if the child has ADHD and which presentation of symptoms they are showing.

Causes of ADHD

Misconceptions surrounding the causes of ADHD dominate the internet and opinions alike. Some believe the disorder is caused by eating too much sugar, while others believe it comes from watching too much television. Some blame socioeconomic factors, such as poverty and family chaos. Some people believe that parents are to blame, and that if they raised the child in a different way, the child would not have ADHD. Regardless of how

41

believable these arguments are, they are not true, and ADHD is not caused by trivial matters such as watching television and sugar. In some cases, these things don't make the symptoms better, but they are not the cause.

The reason why the causes of ADHD have not yet been definitively defined is because research is still being undertaken. The disorder is still new to the medical community, and no one knows what causes ADHD or what the risk factors are. In spite of this, there are theories and conclusions made by those who have authority in the field. The International Consensus Statement provides 208 evidence-based conclusions about the disorder. This was done to reduce stigma against those affected with the disorder, which often delays treatment (Faraone et al., 2021).

A conclusion that is imperative to narrowing down the cause of ADHD is the understanding that it is not caused by a single genetic or environmental risk factor. A majority of cases of ADHD are caused by the combined effects of many genetic and environmental risks, each having a very small effect (Faraone et al., 2021). Furthermore, more research is being done as to whether or not the following could be possible causes and risk factors: brain injury, premature delivery, low birth weight, use of alcohol and tobacco during pregnancy, and exposure to environmental risks such as lead while pregnant (Centers for Disease Control and Prevention, 2018).

Genetics

Some people wonder if ADHD can be passed down from generation to generation. More specifically, can it run in the family? Research shows the relative risk of ADHD in first degree relatives is between 4.0 and 9.0 (Faraone et al., 2021). If we compare the familial risk of ADHD with other diseases, it is higher than rheumatoid arthritis but lower than schizophrenia. It is possible for disorders to cluster amongst families because they share environments and genes. Therefore, there is strong evidence that a contributing factor to ADHD is genes (Anita, 2009).

Brain Development

Questions have been asked on whether brain development has something to do with the development of ADHD in a child's brain. The American Academy of Child & Adolescent Psychiatry (AACAP) offers some explanation on how brain development relates to ADHD and if it causes it. Some of the areas in the brain of children with ADHD are smaller than those of their peers without the disorder. The AACAP (2019) explains that ADHD is a disorder that affects the frontal lobe area of the brain, which is the part of the brain that is responsible for planning, memory, impulse control, judgment, planning, and the ability to delay gratification, along with other tasks. The frontal lobe of those with ADHD may develop later than the frontal lobe of their peers who don't have ADHD.

The brain consists of nerve cells called neurons that transmit signals. Groups of nerve cells are called networks and these networks are how signals in the brain travel. The networks that work differently in people with ADHD are those that function in reward, focus, planning, attention, shifting between tasks, and movement (ADHD & the Brain, 2019). Neurotransmitters are chemicals that assist in transmitting signals between nerve cells via the networks. Dopamine and norepinephrine are two neurotransmitters that research shows play a role in ADHD.

In spite of all this research and knowledge on brain development and ADHD, scientists are still unable to pinpoint how this causes ADHD. What is known is that brain development has a bearing on ADHD, but it is not yet known how exactly it causes the disorder.

Environmental Risk Factors

Although genetics and brain development may have a contributing factor on someone who develops ADHD, those are not definitive causes of the disorder. We have to consider environmental risk factors and potential gene-environment interactions. Some of these risk factors include food additives, lead contamination during pregnancy, cigarette and alcohol exposure, maternal smoking during pregnancy, and low birth weight. These may put the child at greater risk to develop ADHD (Banerjee et al., 2007).

Forms of Distress Related to ADHD

Children are aware of certain diseases. They understand what it means to get sick and to take medication to help heal an illness. ADHD may be harder to explain to a child who is affected by the disorder. The child may feel continued dread, especially when the parent is reacting negatively to their diagnosis. The child may go through periods of depression, self-loathing, and self-blame. In extreme cases, they may resort to self-harm or even an attempt on their life. The child may develop negative responses to their diagnosis and lose their self-worth and self-esteem. The breakdown of the family may also lead the child to think that it is at their fault that all these bad things are happening. The child may feel as if the world would be better off without them.

Due to a person developing negative emotions towards themselves, they may struggle to maintain their physical health. If a person is in distress due to their ADHD, they may be seen to forgo exercise medication as well as maintaining an unhealthy, imbalanced diet. Being in a negative mental space that contains stress and anxiety will leave you unmotivated to care for yourself, which may be the gateway to other health issues and the worsening of other ADHD symptoms. In worst-case scenarios, psychosis, hallucinations, and paranoia can also occur.

Research shows that children living with ADHD are more likely to be exposed to stressful conditions. This is because ADHD is often misunderstood, and parents may feel frustrated with a child who is suffering from the disorder. The child may be having difficulty at school, as well as the family struggling to cope with finances and the emotionally supporting the disorder demands. ADHD creates a stressful environment for the child with their disorder and their family.

Hartman et al. (2019) hypothesized that "high exposure to stress relates to a more persistent and complex (i.e., multi-problem) form of ADHD, while low-stress exposure relates to remitting ADHD over the course of adolescence." They found that high stressors in someone who has ADHD will either cause severe and persistent emotion dysregulation (irritability, extreme reactivity, frustration) or elevated and increasing irritability, anxiety, and depression. Lower stress levels mean remitting ADHD and decreasing internalizing and externalizing problems. Stressors need to be taken into account when diagnosing and prescribing treatment for ADHD. The child may not need therapy alone; perhaps the family will need it too.

CHAPTER 4

THE PSYCHOLOGY OF A CHILD WITH

ADHD

Rachel got Harvey the help he needed as soon as she felt like something was wrong with him. His pain was evident because his inability to regulate his emotions was intense. Even then, there is no way for Rachel to know or even understand what Harvey feels, because he's a child and may have difficulty articulating his feelings. How can a parent empathize with their child who has ADHD if they don't understand how and what they feel? To understand the psychology of a child with ADHD is to provide insight that may better equip a parent with the tools to be more compassionate to their child.

Difficulty Expressing and Communicating Distress

Language and communication doesn't only include spoken language, but also nonverbal communication. The way ADHD affects the brain undermines communication. When the child begins to interrupt others, blurt out answers, and overpower the conversation, it is because of these ADHD symptoms. They are not able to have a coherent conversation where one point is connected to another, so it may seem like their conversation is sporadic because none of the points are organized or related.

Another disorder that affects communication like ADHD is autism. In this disorder, the children are unable to break down social cues and understand them adequately. It's a small similarity, but with autism, the communication and developmental delays affect a large area of the child's social life. To remedy these difficulties in communication, adults are supposed to adjust their communication style as much as possible to get to the same level of the child and enable easier communication. These kinds of difficulties with communication should be taken into consideration when it is noticed that the child is having a harder time expressing themselves when they are in distress.

It has been established that children with ADHD are unable to regulate their emotions, but this difficulty can manifest in different ways. A child may have an explosive meltdown or outburst when they are feeling angry or stressed. Alternatively, others may lack motivation to do something when they're bored. A child with ADHD may experience frustration in the face of minor annoyance, worrying too much for too long about minor things, being unable to calm down when angry or upset, feeling wounded if given gentle criticism, and feeling urgency to get something they want at that very moment.

The child with ADHD lacks sufficient executive functions and is unable to put things into perspective and manage how they respond to situations they find themselves in. A child with ADHD may experience emotions much more intensely, to the point where they may feel overwhelmed, frustrated, discouraged, or give up too quickly or avoid interaction with others. It is almost like an emotional sensory overload. If so much is coming so fast, it will be hard to sort and articulate those feelings, which is even more true when it comes to feelings of distress. Worsening ADHD symptoms can be attributed to stress, meaning a child with ADHD will struggle to articulate themselves when they are in distress (Brown, n.d.).

ADHD Triggers

When we consider other types of mental disorders, such as PTSD or trauma, we can see that triggers can come at any time and in any shape and form. Both the child and the parents need to be fully aware of what it is that sets off the child's symptoms. Triggers can come from any direction and at varied intensities, which can cause the child's reactions to differ. ADHD can cause a child to live a life that is filled with anxiety, so if it's triggered regularly, it becomes a real issue that needs to be addressed.

Is the child okay one moment and having an episode of rage the next? Do their ADHD symptoms come out of nowhere, or do they come after being triggered by something? Most parents feel as if they come from nowhere, but if they pay attention, they will notice a pattern. It is believed that there are certain things that trigger the onset of ADHD symptoms. As to what triggers each person, the causes are different. There are different biological and environmental factors that can trigger the onset of ADHD symptoms. If Rachel was aware of what set Harvey off, she could have avoided it. These are the theories as to what could trigger the symptoms of ADHD including lifestyle situations.

Mineral Deficiencies

Mineral deficiencies, such as a zinc deficiency, can cause ADHD-like symptoms, causing a child to feel restless, become inattentive, and lag behind in their cognitive development. Some research indicates that children with ADHD have lower than normal zinc levels (Lillis, 2019). Although there's no conclusive evidence to suggest mineral deficiencies cause ADHD, a direct link has been established between taking zinc supplements and improved symptoms of ADHD.

Food Additives

More research has to be done in this regard, but it is believed that certain food additives may exacerbate symptoms of ADHD. A link has been made between artificial food colors (AFCs) and ADHD. AFCs are believed to cause hyperactivity, impulsivity, and inattention. On top of that, the symptoms caused by AFCs affected children the same way, whether or not they had ADHD.

Lack of Sleep

Some medications of ADHD are stimulants that increase dopamine in certain areas of the brain. Increased dopamine levels goes a long way to alleviate ADHD symptoms. Unfortunately, because the medication is a stimulant, it can cause sleep disturbances, meaning a child who is prescribed these stimulants may have difficulty falling asleep and wake frequently throughout the night. Lack of sleep causes fatigue and makes the child feel lethargic, which will aggravate ADHD symptoms. The child who lacks sleep may become more inattentive, indecisive, and impulsive. If possible, medications for ADHD that are stimulants should not be taken before bedtime to avoid sleep disturbances (Lillis, 2019).

Media and Technology

There has been no conclusive evidence that media and technology increase the symptoms of ADHD, but the studies that have been done found a significant relationship between excessive media and technology use and ADHD behaviors. Of course, further research needs to be done to find out what kind of effect media and technology has on ADHD. There are various theories surrounding ADHD and media, one being that fast-paced, graphic violence media may cause arousal in children who have

ADHD. Another theory is that problems with attentiveness arise when parents don't limit screen time and children become overstimulated from the phone, television, and personal computer screens.

Completing Tasks That Require Concentration

Using executive functions, including tasks like completing homework or learning a new skill, is something that requires a certain level of concentration. The three core executive functions that a child with ADHD struggles with are inhibitory control, working memory, and cognitive flexibility. Children with ADHD struggle with executive functions, so completing tasks that require concentration may seem like it causes ADHD symptoms for them, when it actually makes them more apparent (Lillis, 2019).

Easily Distracted

Children who have been diagnosed with ADHD have been described as those who don't listen or are easily distracted. This is because not only can the minds of those children not keep focus, they are also unable to control their focus. If a student in a classroom has ADHD, it is better that the student sit closer to the teacher to avoid distractions. The further away from the teacher they are, the more they will be at risk of being distracted by something outside the window, their friends, or just their own thoughts.

The brain of a child with ADHD is unable to screen distraction, as it has a lower level of brain arousal. Noise outside, something in the hallway, or the child's own emotions and thoughts are things that their brain should screen out, but is unable to. This is why the brain can't remain focused. If the activity is not engaging enough, the child will definitely lose focus. As previously mentioned, tasks that require mental effort aren't the favorite of a child who has this disorder. Teachers and parents may feel this is a child acting out on purpose by not listening or losing focus so easily. "If children could pay better attention, they would" (ADDitude Editors, 2009).

Anger Flare Ups

When Rachel decided to get Harvey help, it was because of a flare up. Harvey was not responding well to following instructions, and thereafter received a light reprimand followed by an educational punishment. Harvey, as is the case with many other children who have ADHD, could not control his emotions. He began to cry and scream, and spiral into a hysterical fire of rage. Once Harvey began his explosive episode, neither Rachel nor Mike could calm him down; it seemed Harvey's emotions had free reign, and there was nothing anyone could do to calm them down.

A child with ADHD feels emotions more intensely than other children who don't have ADHD. They also have a hard time regulating those emotions and keeping things in perspective. It's not as if the child is doing this on purpose, but it needs to be understood that with ADHD comes anger and frustration. The child is emotional and on edge most of the time, and even the smallest thing can tip those emotions over to anger. ADHD is a disorder that causes the child to be in a constant state of distress, which is why anger is so easy to come by.

When a child with ADHD explodes, it is because they are trying to make sense of their intense emotions. Perhaps Harvey wanted to tell his mother that he was not trying to be bad, he just felt the urge to keep going and that no matter what, he could not stop himself. Harvey is unable to naturally curb his liveliness, but even so, no child wants to be bad on purpose. If he could, he probably would have explained that he just wanted to play and that he could not complete the educational punishment because it was hard to focus on one task for a long time. Instead of being clear and concise about his feelings, they manifest as a jumbled-up intensity that bursts through as anger.

As previously stated, a child with ADHD can't regulate their emotions, being possibly unable to identify and articulate them. It follows that they will not be able to communicate that they are feeling overwhelmed. A child with ADHD will struggle to put into words that they are feeling anxious because they cannot make sense of what they feel. Harvey will not be able to express to his mother that he is feeling frustrated because he can't do things as well as his peers, or that he seems to always be getting into trouble. ADHD in children is particularly difficult because children are still developing, and they may have difficulty expressing themselves even if they do not have ADHD. The take away from this is that a child with ADHD wants to express that they are not doing it on purpose, and that they cannot speak about how anxious, depressed, and overwhelmed they feel.

CHAPTER 5

MAJOR DIFFICULTIES AND STRENGTHS

OF A CHILD WITH ADHD

A child with ADHD may have difficulties navigating normal life, but they are more gifted than they are given credit for. They may not be able to do school work uninterrupted, or be able to focus on one task to completion, but there are two sides to the coin. With the difficulties they experience, there are also strengths that they possess. These children are not write-offs or useless, their brains simply work differently. If their thought processes are understood, it's easier to understand where their strengths lie. Identifying the difficulties and strengths that ADHD brings out in a child will help parents and teachers bring out more of the strengths and support the child through their difficulties.

A childhood is primarily spent at school and at home, with various social interactions in-between. From Monday to Friday, a child can spend up to eight hours a day at school, learning and partaking in extracurricular activities. It's not unusual for ADHD to be detected at school by the child's educators. After school, as well as on the weekends, the child spends their time at home with their family and friends. If a child has ADHD, these two settings are where the disorder will wreak havoc, as the child will develop difficulties in both locations. What will these difficulties look like? What will the strengths look like?

Difficulties at Home

The home environment is one of relaxation and leisure, and children are their most comfortable in their home environment. Although the home is a place of rest, children are expected to do chores and behave a certain way. Depending on the household, a child may be expected to clean their room, clean the house, partake in doing the laundry, and washing dishes, as well as cooking meals for the family. There is some responsibility placed on a child to perform communal tasks in the home. These chores invoice executive functions, and because of this, a family who has a child with ADHD as a member is likely to witness the child display some difficulties in being a functioning member of the family.

Emotional Distress

When the child is at home, they tend to let loose and be who they really are. They can let down their guard and freely express how they feel or show what they are going through. However, ADHD can stunt that ability. Instead of the child being able to express themselves about any frustration or confusion that they are experiencing in their lives, they may appear moody, angsty, and unwilling to be an enthusiastic participant in family activities. This can cause emotional distress amongst parents and siblings alike, creating tension in the home and robbing it of that peaceful atmosphere it is supposed to have.

If a child has a younger sibling, but is experiencing ADHD symptoms, they may not be able to be that guiding older influences that their sibling needs them to be. We all have a role to play within the nuclear family structure, but ADHD can cripple a child in a way that they are too distressed to take part in regular duties within the family. This type of emotional stress may mean that a younger sibling is left to their own devices.

A child with ADHD may become resented by their siblings because they are perceived to hog the attention of the parents. They obviously will need more attention, but that doesn't mean that the children and the siblings are less deserving. Unfortunately for the family, including the spouse, the child with ADHD will take up all the attention of the parents and will seemingly dominate the home life of the entire family. The child's siblings will have to learn how to be independent and self-reliant, forcing them to grow up at a much more accelerated pace.

Difficulty with Organization and Order

Difficulty getting organized is one of the more prominent difficulties experienced at home. There is already chaos in the brain of a child with ADHD, and because they deal with a lot internally, they are sometimes unable to keep organized externally. A child with ADHD will have issues taking out their uniform and getting themselves ready for school; their room may look like a bomb hit due to the fact that clothes, toys, and books are not adequately organized. Lack of organization will stop the child from being able to wash, rinse, and dry dishes in an efficient manner. This difficulty of staying organized will be frustrating for parents, as the child will not be able to perform any tasks in an organized manner and this may cause disruption in the home life of the family. The child may have to be monitored closely to ensure they remain on top of doing things in a systematic way.

Distraction

Focus is outlined in a previous chapter as something that is elusive to a child with ADHD. Research shows that a child with ADHD experiences a lower level of brain arousal, which is why they are easily distracted by internal and external stimuli. Sustained mental effort is at the crux of the issue. These types of children are quite often easily distracted and can be found daydreaming, distracted by external stimuli or their own internal thoughts. If they are not sufficiently stimulated by the chore at hand, they will lose focus, which is needed in the pursuit of tasks within the home. When a parent is talking to the child, they want to feel as if the child is paying attention and listening to what the parent is saying. Often parents may feel their child has their head in the clouds, as they are never focused on what they are being told or unable to fully focus on a task at hand. The child is able to pay attention, but unable to control it.

Forgetting or Losing Objects

Forgetting things is listed as one of the symptoms of ADHD, as per the DSM-5. This problem arises because of a few other difficulties mentioned above. The inattentive child will be functioning on autopilot a majority of the time because the brain is not really focused on what is happening. When the brain is not focused on each and every move that is made, it is easy to forget where something was placed. While the child with ADHD is packing their school bag, they may be thinking about the homework of the day, and therefore may not remember that they put their eye glasses in the side pocket. Later, when the child has to do their homework or reading, they will not know where they placed their glasses. Being unable to keep organized also plays a role in the child losing items or forgetting where they were put. This can cause disruption in the home when a parent has requested their child to put something away and they become unable to recall it when it is needed at a later time. This is even more frustrating if it is an important item, like car keys or a wallet.

Difficulties at School

The school environment is not as relaxed as the home environment, being more formal because learning takes place there. Most of the learning done at school is structured and inflexible. Lessons are planned and are delivered to children by their teachers. The pace of learning is determined by the majority, and teachers expect the children to be able to cope and keep up. Children are also expected to keep themselves well-behaved and organized. This environment is not relaxed like the home environment, and there are legitimate expectations placed on the child.

Unfortunately, not every child flourishes in the school environment, even under normal circumstances. If the child has ADHD, however, their life at school is a living hell. School requires of every child everything that ADHD has robbed them of. For example, school requires a child to apply long levels of mental concentration and sit still to receive the knowledge that the educator has for them. Children with ADHD are often mislabeled as disruptive and bad because they are unable to conform to the classroom setting. The disorder can make it difficult for such a child to prosper academically.

Difficulty Maintaining Focus on a Task

When a child with ADHD has difficulty focusing, it can cause difficulties at school. Not only will the child disrupt their own learning, but they will disrupt the classroom as well. When a child is unable to focus on a task to completion, it may not get completed, which will adversely affect the child's assessment. Focusing on a task could be class work, assignments, or graded assessments. If a child is struggling to maintain focus, they will not get the full educational value behind that task. Teachers who are unaware that the child has a disorder may think that the child is academically lacking, when in actual fact, they simply need extra attention. The child's academic assessments may not be a true reflection of their capabilities.

Easily Distracted

A child with ADHD has a low arousal rate and is more likely to be distracted by internal thoughts and external stimuli. This means that this child should not be sitting at the back or close to a window. Instead, the child must sit at the front, where the teacher is able to reign them in and recapture their attention and bring their focus back to learning. The child can only focus for a short time, which is why they can be easily distracted. Concentration is required to follow the lessons for each day; inability to concentrate on a lesson and getting easily distracted will result in the child not receiving the true value of the education being offered.

Constant Reminders

Due to the fact that the child is unable to focus and is easily distracted, they will need constant attention and reminders from their educators. It is disruptive for the educator and the classroom environment as a whole to have to keep reminding one, or a few students, to sit still or pay attention and concentrate. In a situation where the child is not yet diagnosed with ADHD, they may be constantly reprimanded and scolded for having to be constantly reminded what to do or how to behave. Even when the disorder is diagnosed and educators have been made aware, it is still a disruption in the class to chase after one student, especially if the educator has not been trained on how to effectively teach children with ADHD. Some educators will follow through on the constant reminders for the child with ADHD, but not all of them can.

Avoiding Long Tasks

Being in school requires many different tasks and responsibilities. When the child is young, long tasks are few and far between. As the school years pass by, however, the child may have to focus on longer tasks and apply their concentration for a longer period of time. An example is exams and study periods. There are few exams at six years old, but by twelve, there may be more than a couple of papers to sit through. The child with ADHD will have to not only sit through the various assessments and exams, but they will have to also spend hours preparing for them by studying. Difficulties arise when the child has to perform these tasks because, as discussed in a previous chapter, the child with ADHD is unable to perform long tasks. They will most likely avoid them, but some are compulsory and crucial to the learning experience.

Hurriedness and Distracting Errors

The child with ADHD has been described as one who seems to be on the go, constantly, as if they are being operated by a motor. They rush through because they don't know how to be calm or slow down. Tasks at school require deliberate attention and being meticulous in order to avoid making errors. If a child is not able to regulate behavior and emotions, they won't be able to stop rushing and slow themselves down. Hurriedness will lead to carelessness, which can in turn lead to glaring errors that will disadvantage the child and score them lower marks.

Difficulty with Memory Exercises

Working memory is when a person uses their short-term memory to perform tasks. In the classroom, the class can read a story and then be asked to answer the questions set out in their textbook that relate to the story. In a scenario like this, a child will be forced to rely on their short-term memory to answer the questions. A child with ADHD has no issues with their short or long-term memory, but issues arise when they have to use their working memory. Applying their short-term memory to perform tasks is something they struggle with. If the child is undiagnosed, it won't be known that this is an area that they struggle with. Their educators won't know that this child could be taught how to improve their working memory, and they will likely fail at tasks that require working memory (Raspolich, n.d.).

Difficulty with Metacognitive Processes and Problem Solving

Metacognition is defined as being aware of one's own cognitive processes, usually involving a conscious attempt to control them. A child with ADHD has poor or lacking skills when it comes to cognitive abilities because they struggle with perception, learning, memory, understanding, awareness, reasoning, judgment, intuition, and language. When the child is unable to control their cognitive processes, then their school work and classroom experience will be negatively affected. Executive functions have been fingered as another difficulty children with ADHD have, as problem solving is a part of the executive functions.

Problem-solving is a part of every subject at school because life is problem-solving, from the mathematical one plus one to the language exercises in English class. To test if a child has adequately absorbed the knowledge presented to them, they will need to solve problems that require them to apply their knowledge. The child with ADHD is unable to do that, due to lacking working memory skills and executive functions. This inability will cause issues for them at school, because they won't be able to apply the information they have been given.

Language Difficulties

The communication medium used at school is mostly spoken word in a language that everyone within the classroom understands. The definition of language is based on language modalities: being expressive, being receptive, and the domains of language structure (vocabulary, grammar, and discourse) (Edwards, n.d.). Language difficulties are used to cover a broad spectrum of language problems. The cause is still unclear, but children with ADHD have been known to have language difficulties. "Sciberras et al., found large deficits in language functioning in children with ADHD across all language modalities" (Edwards, n.d.). In a classroom, the child must be both vocal and receptive to language, as well as be able to put that to paper. This will greatly impair the child's learning experience because they need language to communicate.

Difficulty Relating to Adults and Peers

School is a formal environment where learning takes place, but it also has a social aspect to it. Not only do the children sit together in class, they also have recess where they go outside and play. Depending on the school, the playground may have swings, jungle gyms, and slides. This social aspect of school means that the student has to play and relate to peers and teachers the entire day, but language difficulties and being unable to regulate one's emotions may be a hindrance to being able to relate with one's peers. Without the necessary social interactions, it is hard for a child to develop adequately.

Strengths

A child with ADHD will experience difficulties at home and at school, but that's not because they have a learning impairment, but because they experience performance impairments. Therefore, they may have the same intellectual capacity as anyone else. The child need only be coached in coping strategies for them to reinforce deficient areas for their strengths to flourish. Of course, not all children with ADHD have the same strengths, but all of them need to be taught how to turn lemons into lemonade by making aspects of their condition an advantage instead of a disadvantage.

Creativity

It is not uncommon to hear that a child with ADHD is creative. The child may struggle with logical tasks that require focus or increased levels of concentration, but the opposite is true for creativity. Their brains are wired differently than the average child, meaning they have a different view of the world and its problems. This different view may likely lead to a creative outlook on life. When encouraged, these children will gain more confidence in this strength and be unashamed to express their different way of thinking.

Innovation

When a child continually faces trouble because their mind doesn't function like the minds of children their age, normal everyday tasks are daunting, and their mind doesn't respond normally according to societal expectations, they tend to become creative in their approach to life. This creativity often morphs to innovation. How are tasks performed in an easier way? How can things that are hated turned into more interesting tasks? A child living with ADHD can be an inventive thinker simply because of the difficulties the disorder causes in their lives.

Intuition

Children with ADHD are described as being intuitive. They are often highly sensitive beings who are in touch with what others may be feeling without the person expressing themselves. This intuition superpower may make a child with ADHD more empathetic and kind; they will lean toward love and showing compassion for others. The regular brain has to filter and sort incoming sensations to manageable chunks for the brain to process, but sometimes some key details are filtered out. The sensory overload that comes with ADHD is terrible, but it can also provide added information that is primarily ignored by the regular brain.

Curiosity and Energy

ADHD can make a child fidgety or restless. They seem like they can't keep still and are always moving on to the next thing, but this is not always a bad thing. Being so full of energy can be used as an advantage once the child is taught how to manage this symptom. Furthermore, their curiosity for life is piqued because they live in a completely different world. A child with ADHD still has the curiosity to explore what life has in store for them.

CHAPTER 6

ADHD - ADDITIONAL PROBLEMS AND

SOLUTIONS

ADHD does not exist in a vacuum. The children that have this disorder live in the real world in real-life scenarios. Sometimes, the situation of the child and the family is dire and aggravates the symptoms of ADHD. Regardless of the circumstances, the parent or caregiver will have to use practical skills and tips to deal with the child. Theories on how to treat a child with ADHD or what a parent needs to understand does not fully empower them on what to do when faced with different scenarios, but it does help them be practical and specific about a way to cope and deal with these children.

Rachel's scenario is one where Harvey was more likely to thrive. Rachel and Mike are married, and Harvey is their only child. Their home is one where they are financially stable and the spouses are supportive of one another. Rachel has the luxury to quit her job and focus on Harvey and his presentation of ADHD. Harvey has the advantage of having a parent who is dedicated to understanding his disorder and finding a way to make it better. Rachel has no distractions, and will be able to make an effective change to Harvey's life quite quickly. It will be easier to integrate the methods and techniques at school, as Rachel will be able to communicate her findings to Harvey's teachers.

Not all families who are affected by ADHD are able to deal with the disorder this efficiently. Rachel, Harvey, and Mike's situation is the best kind you can have. Not all mother's can quit their jobs to focus on their child's disorder: some mothers or fathers are single parents who have to work more than one job to support their family. Other families have more than one child to pay attention to. Some children don't even have families at all, and in that case, who will help them adjust and deal with their ADHD? For each situation, a parent or caregiver must have specific actions to take to assist in dealing with the symptoms of ADHD.

ADHD - Adopted Children

Adoption is already a difficult situation to deal with. Loving parents may adopt an orphaned child and give the child all they love they have to give, but things do not fall into place seamlessly at the snap of a finger. It takes years of hard work and sometimes therapy to integrate an adopted child into the family. Even then, just like normal families, it is not perfect. Things become more difficult when the child has ADHD. Although stress is not the cause of ADHD, we are aware that earlier environmental stressors on a pregnant woman can affect the developing brain of the fetus, possibly leading to the child presenting ADHD symptoms in their toddler phase or later. A pregnant woman giving up her baby is usually a situation that is enveloped in stress, meaning the child is predisposed to develop the disorder.

After giving birth, a nursing mother is inseparable from their newborn. Even if she is unable to nurse her baby, the skin-to-skin affection the child receives is paramount to its survival. Children separated from their mothers at birth due to the decision of the mother to put the child up for adoption can result in major alterations in dopamine and other neurotransmitters, which may contribute to the development of ADHD. An adopted child has to battle with feeling out of place, low self-esteem, and the stigma that comes with being adopted. Parents of adopted children need to be aware of the feelings of adopted children so they are able to tackle their ADHD from a place of compassion and understanding.

Be Honest

A parent to an adopted child who has ADHD should never downplay anything. The circumstances of the child's adoption should be told to the child, and the parents should answer any questions the child has surrounding their adoption or their birth parents honestly. Honesty around their ADHD should also be expressed. The child should be told that their brain works differently, but that it is not inferior to other children's brains. Honesty breeds trust, and that is the most important thing to build between a parent and their adopted child. The child should be included in any decisions about their disorder so that the parents are demonstrating openness and honesty with the child. Furthermore, when the parent is honest with the adopted child, they are less likely to allow bullies or false information to be spread about them at school or on the playground. Honesty will pave a path of self-love and self-confidence because the child will have a sense of identity, as well as knowing what is going on in terms of their disorder.

Offer Reassurance

Adoptive parents will need to constantly reassure adopted children. When a child is adopted, they may feel like they do not belong to their new family. Their mannerisms and character may be different from the members of their new home, which will reduce their sense of belonging. If they present with ADHD symptoms, this may further reinforce how different they are to their adoptive family. Parents must make a deliberate effort to offer reassurance at all times; the child must be reminded that they are different and not less than others, and that they are loved and have a place in the family. The child must be praised and told how proud they make their adoptive parents, and that they bring joy and light to the world. The child should be reminded that they can do anything they put their mind to. It is important to emphasize that even if the child had a rough start to life, it does not mean they will fail, success is still within reach (Kessler, 2015).

Prepare the Child for the World

Unfortunately, the world is not always a kind place. Adopted children may have passed through the hands of numerous families, meaning they may already harbor resentment toward the world and the fact that they were given up for adoption or the death of their parents put them in that position. In spite of this unfortunate beginning to life, the world may continue to be harsh to adoptees who have ADHD. They may face constant stigma and teasing, or be labeled as unwanted or bad. As parents, it is important to desensitize the child to what they could face out in the world. Let them know the stigma they will face because they are adopted and because they have ADHD. Afterwards, reinforce the fact that these criticisms are baseless, and that they are special, capable, and loved.

ADHD - Children who Have Experienced Trauma

The APA Dictionary of Psychology (n.d.) defines trauma as "any disturbing experience that results in significant fear, helplessness, dissociation, confusion, or other disruptive feelings intense enough to have a long-lasting negative effect on a person's attitudes, behavior, and other aspects of functioning." The stress that occurs from trauma can worsen the effects of ADHD. The part of the brain that trauma impacts may also increase inattentiveness, impulsiveness, hyperactiveness, and social and learning difficulties, as well as other co-occurring disorders. Parents of children who have trauma need to be cognizant of ways to deal with both the child's ADHD and trauma.

A differentiation between symptoms of ADHD and PTSD should be made, because the symptoms often overlap. ADHD is considered an inheritable disorder that is characterized by attention deficits and lack of behavioral control, while PTSD is not inherited because it is experienced after trauma, and it is characterized by hyper vigilant behavior and re-experiencing of the trauma. ADHD causes functional limitations, while PTSD causes changes in how a person deals with external stressors (Brown, 2020). Trauma does not alleviate the symptoms of ADHD, and may potentially make them worse, meaning parents must know how to deal with a child that is dealing with trauma and ADHD.

Supportive Family Environment

There are multiple ways to lessen the effects of trauma and toxic effects in children that have ADHD, and that includes having a supportive loving family environment that is also buttressed by an inclusive community. When the parents of a child who has ADHD and trauma include other adults in knowing the child's trauma triggers, as well as their ADHD triggers, it is easier to deal with and support the child through their symptoms. The goal is to provide a safe and stable space for the child, both at home and at school, to ensure that the triggers of their trauma are suppressed. This way, they don't accidentally aggravate the child's ADHD symptoms.

Nurturing Parenting Skills

A child who has experienced trauma will not benefit from a parent who is harsh and hard in their disciplining. In order to nurture a child who has trauma, a parent will need to employ a gentle tone, as well as practicing compassion and understanding when the child's trauma is triggered. The child's triggers should be learned, as should methods that best calm the child down so that parents know how to respond if and when the child becomes triggered. Parents must maximize making the child feel safe and comfortable within their surroundings, and ensure that the child knows that they can always confide in the parent, even when their trauma comes to surface.

Parents Educated on Trauma

There is a saying that 'if you know better, you do better', and the same applies to trauma. The parent of a child who has trauma will not know how to deal with the trauma if they don't know what trauma is; how will they help the child if they don't know how people with trauma react in situations where they are reliving it? Educating themselves on trauma and how it presents itself, as well as how it relates to ADHD, will provide parents the skills needed in order to be empathetic and help them know how to respond to their child when their trauma exposes itself. Being a part of a community or support group of parents who have children that have trauma will also create networks of support for those parents, and give them adequate knowledge on how to better support their children (Brown, 2020).

Adequate Access to Health Care and Social Services

A parent of a child with trauma is unable to diagnose the trauma or psychologically understand the triggers of the child and how to cope with that. The family will need counseling and support from the psychiatric field, which is usually provided free of charge in most countries. The child themselves would have to be provided with support in the form of therapy so that they can unpack their trauma and understand why it is debilitating to them. Meanwhile, the parents need to make sure that the child has access to these services so that they can have the best path to recovery. Trauma is best dealt with with the support of the medical profession, and victims of trauma may sometimes need prescriptions or medication for a short time or for the rest of their lives in order to restore their quality of life. The child who has trauma may also need to join support groups in order to partake in the group therapy and improve their chances at disarming their trauma (Brown, 2020).

ADHD - Children who Have Experienced Parental Separation

Parents with children that have ADHD have the responsibility to provide them with a stable home environment. However, situations like the one Rachel and Mike have provided for Harvey are the exception to the rule. Unfortunately, life is not that utopian, and parental separation occurs at a much higher rate than ten or twenty years ago. When families break up, this creates stress that may aggravate the symptoms of ADHD. The parents must be cognizant of the effect that the separation will have on the child and the household as a whole. If the parent who doesn't have primary custody is willing to spend time with the children, then there will be two households in which the child will spend their time. Parents need to be aware of how to lessen the impact of this major transition on a child that is diagnosed with ADHD (Rosen, n.d.).

Plan

Parents that are separating need to have a plan on what is going to happen going forward. Although the parents would have separated, they need to present a united front for the child who has ADHD and show them that, although they are separating, they are still on the same side and that they still love the child unconditionally. The parents need to agree on what's in the challenge is to be told about the separation and about what will change going forward. As with most separations, the child may feel like they are losing control of the whole situation, so parents need to reassure them and make them feel safe. An important thing to stress when parents are sitting down to talk to their child is to reaffirm that a separation is not due to the child's special needs or their disorder.

Prepare the Child

Children with ADHD already experience feelings of being overwhelmed and confused, so it is important to prepare your child for what is to come. The parents can talk about what it means to separate and what will come as a result of this separation so that events that come do not surprise or bombard the child. The parents do not need to tell the child about things that may happen years from that point; they can give the child a breakdown of what is to happen in the coming weeks, such as the fact that their father will be moving out to a new apartment and that they will likely spend a few nights there every week. As things develop, parents should alert their child of further changes, and discuss how they will affect their new family structure.

Stay Consistent

Inconsistency may aggravate the symptoms of a child who has ADHD, as it is a stressor. Going between two different environments that have different rules may create an unstable life for a child with ADHD. Therefore, it is important to keep the rules consistent whether they are visiting their mother or their father so that they can keep the same structure. If bedtime at the mother's house is at 8 p.m., then bedtime at the father's house should also be at 8 p.m. The reward system that the parents had been using prior to the separation should remain the same; parents should not feel the need to overcompensate for their absence with gifts. Stability will reduce the symptoms of ADHD, which is the overall goal that should be maintained throughout the separation. Staying consistent also applies to protecting rituals and schedules, such as school pick-up and drop-off times and birthday and holiday traditions.

Dating

A parent who has gone through a separation has every right to move on and begin dating whenever they feel ready. It is important, however, to be mindful of dating when you have a child with ADHD. Children with ADHD struggle to form connections to begin with, so it is difficult to introduce a new person within the home. The child sees their home as a safe place where they can be themselves and feel at ease, and introducing a new person in the child's safe space can increase the child's anxiety and cause them to resent this new person. This added stress might amplify the child's frustration, as well as confusion as to what this new person is doing in their home. The child may feel panic if they feel that your new partner is there to try to be their other parent.

Unfortunately, having a child with ADHD means that any spouse chosen will have to understand that this is a large part of your life, and that they will need to help with it as well. If the parent's partner does not accept the child's ADHD, it can make the child feel rejected and unwanted. A parent can be heartbroken if they find somebody they would like to date, but who is not interested in leading a life that is intertwined with ADHD. It is a heavy load to carry, and if a single parent doesn't find a companion who is willing to take it on, it may lead to depression. When a parent is depressed, they are unable to parent to their best of their ability, meaning the child's ADHD symptoms may worsen.

Dating when you have a child with special needs is very complicated to navigate. We cannot expect single parents who have children with ADHD to put their heads in the sand and focus solely on the needs of the child. To lead a full and happy life, the parent needs to satisfy all their own needs, and that includes the need for companionship if they so wish. Some parents would prefer to remain single, and that is acceptable. If the parent decides that they would love to date, that is also acceptable. What is important is how the relationship will affect the home life of the child. If the relationship has more cons than pros as it relates to the child, then it is not worth pursuing.

There is a possibility that because the parent is frustrated and overwhelmed with dealing with ADHD, they may be desperate for attention from the opposite sex. This could lead to attracting the wrong kind of person, leading to someone who may be abusive toward the parent or child. Introducing your child to a relationship that contributes to their anxiety will lead to a path of destruction. The parents need to make sure that the new partner exhibits healthy traits and is not a toxic person. Toxicity is something that the parent should never tolerate in a potential partner, because if that person can make the parent feel bad about themselves under normal circumstances, then they are likely to put down their child as well, whose well-being is under special circumstances.

If your new partner is introduced to the child too soon, they may develop an unhealthy attachment to the new partner, because the child has experienced a loss in the parent who moved out of the family home. Living with a child who has ADHD is a large responsibility that can overwhelm that child's birth parent. The new partner will quickly feel overwhelmed with their new situation, and if they have negative thoughts then they can easily take it out on the child or the parent, or both. Realizing the full extent of the disorder can also overwhelm the new partner, and they may feel ashamed that that child is their potential step-child. If the new partner disappears or breaks off the relationship, it may cause distress to the child.

Unfortunately, you can never be too sure with dating. Sometimes, a person may feel they picked a suitable partner who is going to support them and the child through their ADHD journey, only to end up being disappointed by that person and feeling like a fool. The parent should never judge themselves for mistakes they make in their dating life. Compassion for themselves, as well as forgiveness for any mistakes that were made, are what the parent should lead with any time they start a new relationship. In all matters of love, a risk needs to be taken in order to see if it will pay off. Therefore, it is important to only introduce new people into the child's life when the relationship is solid and committed.

ADHD - Children who do Not Speak

Research shows that children with ADHD process language differently and are at higher risk for articulation disorders. This means that producing letter sounds is affected and possibly delayed, which may delay a child's ability to speak. Restricted speech could also be as a result of autism or selective mutism that is co-occurring with ADHD. The child's inability to speak may also be due to a nonverbal learning disorder, which is characterized by poor ability of processing nonverbal cues, among other things. Parents with children who have ADHD and who do not speak should do the following:

- Get their child tested for any disability or speech impediment. A parent should never assume what's wrong with the child, and should have professionals assess and diagnose the child based on what the child is experiencing.

- Always wait until it is possible to give the child your full attention so that you are fully able to use all forms of communication (even non-verbal ones, like touch and maintaining eye contact) to try to detect where they are struggling.

ADHD - Children with Attachment Problems

An attachment can be defined as an emotional bond between a child and their parental figure or caregiver. Children who develop attachment issues could do so as a result of a past trauma or separation. According to studies, there's a clear association between ADHD and attachment problems in a child. In order to deal with both the disorder and the attachment problems, parents need to seek medical help for the child. It is not enough to just talk it out as a family, and parents should take the following steps:

1. Seek medical help for the child.
2. Seek training on how to deal with the child's ADHD.

3. Seek training on how to deal with the child attachment problems.

4. Parents should consider that pharmacological treatment may prevent development of attachment problems (Storebø et al., 2013).

ADHD - Young Children (2/4 years old)

ADHD can affect children as young as two years old. At that age, it can be hard to differentiate between ADHD symptoms and normal toddler behavior. It is not called the terrible twos for nothing, as it is common for children between the ages of two and four to have difficulty paying attention following instructions and waiting their turn. Normally, those children outgrow these symptoms, but those children whose symptoms persist will usually be diagnosed with ADHD between the ages of six and 13. A parent with a child who is suspected to have ADHD needs to employ patients and a spirit of compassion, because this child is likely frustrated, confused, and overwhelmed.

Get the Toddler Evaluated

Ignoring the symptoms will not make them go away, and the earlier the child doctor is involved, the better. As stated previously, for a child to be diagnosed with ADHD, the various symptoms must have been present over a period of six months either at home or in the school setting. It is easy to see when a child's symptoms are disruptive either at home or at preschool, because they will be compared with children of the same age. The parent must take the child to their general practitioner, who will then refer them to a child psychiatrist or a pediatrician who will make the initial assessment. The evaluation for children aged between two and four years old should be thorough and follow the guidelines given by the American Academy of Pediatrics and the American Academy of Child and Adolescent Psychiatry.

Parent Behavioral Training

Medication can be recommended for toddlers who are afflicted with ADHD, but parents and caregivers can learn to manage the behavior of preschoolers who have ADHD. The parents will be giving you tools and behavioral techniques needed to effectively deal with the disorder and the child's behavior. This training is designed to help the parents to develop a positive relationship with a child to teach them how they change more, as well as assisting them in managing negative behavior with positive discipline. There are various programs available, but the most common ones are the Triple-P training program (Positive Parenting Program), Incredible Years' parenting program, and parent-child interaction therapy (CHADD, 2018).

ADHD - Capricious Children

A capricious child is one who succumbs to sudden and unaccountable changes of mood or behavior. This was formerly believed to happen because parents usually want to satisfy their child's every whim. Unfortunately, it was believed that satisfying the child's every wish was done at the expense of the development of the child's self-control, obedience, respect for parents and the child's relationship with authority. As a result, a child would become uncontrollable because they didn't know how to wait for good things, meaning they had no discipline and no respect for their parents. A lot of the symptoms of a capricious child could be confused for ADHD symptoms; regardless, parents need to be able to deal with a child who has ADHD and is capricious.

Why is a child considered capricious, and what causes that kind of behavior? Is it simply a parent spoiling their child, or could it be much deeper than that? A child presenting with ADHD could also present with emotional impulsiveness (EI) and deficient emotional self-regulation (DESR). EI deals with emotional regulation, while DESR is concerned with the difficulty or inability to keep in control of the strong emotions that have been provoked. Research has shown that a majority of ADHD cases involve problems with EI and DESR (Barkley, 2020).

Acceptable Behavior

The parents of a child who has ADHD and displays capricious behavior should always give a guideline to the child of what is acceptable and unacceptable behavior. The goal of this is to try to have your child consider the consequences of an action and to control the impulse to act on it. The parent needs to stick to these guidelines and offer punishment where the child deviates. The rules should be simple and clear, and the children should be rewarded for following them. Because the child is still learning, allow some flexibility and don't apply the rules strenuously.

Manage Aggression

Aggressive outbursts may be common among children who have ADHD, and it is important for parents to try to curb this kind of behavior before it escalates and becomes uncontrollable. In order to discourage aggressive outbursts, a parent can employ a timeout, which is an effective way to allow your child to calm down and give them a period to cool off and think about the bad behavior they have been exhibiting. Sometimes, these aggressive outbursts are not exactly the fault of the child, but destructive, abusive, or intentionally harmful behavior which goes against the rules should be punished.

Encourage Exercise

Exercise burns excess energy in healthier ways. A child who has ADHD and exhibits capricious behavior may benefit from exercise, as it helps them to focus their attention on specific movements. Exercise has been known to decrease impulsiveness, improves concentration, reduces the risk of anxiety and depression, and stimulates the brain in healthy ways. Dozens of athletes that play sports professionally have been known to have ADHD. Research shows that exercise is a positive and constructive method through which children with ADHD can focus their passion, attention and energy. Parents should enroll the child in one or more sports at school or extracurricular activity, or the family could take up a sport in which they all play together (Porter, 2017).

ADHD - Children with Speech Impairment

The lack of development of the frontal lobe has been cited as having a bearing on the development of ADHD. Coincidently, the frontal lobe also plays a significant role in speech production, and ADHD also creates language difficulties. Speech impairment by itself does not mean a child has ADHD, but a child with ADHD may have speech impairments. Children who have both ADHD and speech impairment will need to work with speech therapists as well as psychiatrists in order to treat their ADHD and speech impairment.

Speech Therapy

Parents of a child who has ADHD and a speech impairment will need to enroll the child in speech therapy. The APA dictionary of psychology defines speech therapy as the application of remedies, treatment, and counseling for the improvement of speech and language (APA Dictionary of Psychology, n.d.-a). There are specific large body movements that are used during speech therapy sessions that bring the blood and glucose to the frontal lobe of the brain. These movements are recommended by a physical therapist to a speech therapist, and will aid in speech production and language development.

Slowing Down Speech

A child who has ADHD and a speech impairment will often speak too quickly because of cognitive impulsivity related to ADHD. In fact, the child may speak so fast it will sound almost as if the child is slurring. The issue of speaking too quickly can be addressed during a session of speech therapy by having the child draw slow wavy lines as they speak. This is a technique that parents can also employ at home when the child is speaking too fast and their words are borderline incomprehensible (Mac, 2015).

ADHD - Children with Communication Delay

We have spoken at length about the effect that ADHD has on language development as well as speech. Children with ADHD are at a higher risk for language delays; due to the effect of ADHD symptoms, a child will likely lose their train of thought and get off topic when speaking. When a child has language delays, it is hard for them to put thoughts together quickly in linear conversation. These children often also make errors in grammar. These ADHD symptoms may impact the child's capability to communicate. Their listening comprehension can be impaired in noisy situations or in group settings, and the communication delay makes it hard for the child to manage large clumps of conversation in one sitting. Some of these problems are incorrectly diagnosed as auditory processing disorders. However, there is nothing wrong with the actual auditory pathway, because information is able to get in, but the executive function simply impairs the understanding. Dealing with a child with ADHD means that parents will also have to understand their child's communication delays.

In order for parents to adequately deal with the child's communication delays, they need to implement the following:

1. Be patient with the child.

2. Be patient with the learning process on how to deal with a child with communication delays.

3. Do not put pressure on the child to speak.

4. Do not coax or bait the child with phrases like "Can you say..." or "What is this?".

5. Always interact with the child in a calm, playful way so they are comfortable.

ADHD - Hyperactive Children

As previously mentioned, hyperactivity is a condition where the child experiences gross motor activity or restlessness that is excessive for a child of that age. There are various presentations of ADHD and hyperactivity/impulsivity is one of them. This is a presentation of ADHD that can be difficult to cope with because the child can never sit still and is on the go all the time. Parents have to be especially patient with a hyperactive child as they can appear to not listen or have difficulty following instructions. A few tips and techniques can help parents lessen the emotional strain of coping with a hyperactive child.

Establish Order

A hyperactive child needs structure and clarity, and there should be no ambiguity of what is expected of them. A laissez-faire environment where the parents are laid back will not be an environment where the hyperactive child will thrive, as these types of children do not do well in unclear environments. The household should run like clockwork with a clear and established schedule so that the hyperactive child can know what is expected of them every day. To further assist the child in understanding their responsibilities, create a to-do list for them so they can focus on it and not get distracted as the day unfolds. Schedule in unstructured time so the child is able to play outside and just have fun.

Choose Your Battles

Hyperactivity is caused by ADHD. Due to the child's brain chemistry affecting the way signals are transmitted, the child develops a disorder and displays symptoms of hyperactivity. Hyperactivity is not a quirk or a mood, and the child cannot switch it off when they are told to do so. It is important to understand that many of their actions are because they struggle to cope with normal, everyday life. As a parent, you should not fight the child just because they are not acting like every other child their age. A parent should decide what battles are worth fighting and which are just symptoms that the child is displaying and has no control over. Manners are something worth fighting for, but forcing a child to always sit still is not worth the fight.

Minimal Distraction

Children who are hyperactive due to ADHD are very easily distracted. Those distractions can come in the form of internal thoughts, with the child's mind wandering away from the tasks they are supposed to be focused on, or external distractions that can come about by looking out through the window. To counter this, parents need to find somewhere in the home where there is minimal distraction in order to perform tasks. This area needs to be away from any doors or windows, as well as away from loud noises and other people. The parent should explain to the child that they are not being punished, but being protected from distraction.

ADHD - Children with Attention Disorders

Attention disorders can affect children with ADHD. These involve the inability of the child to maintain consistent focus on a task, or difficulties experienced when taking notice of, responding to, or just having an awareness of the behavior or requests of others. It can be hard to cope with a child who has an attention disorder, as parents may feel frustrated with the child's inability to complete tasks in one sitting without constant reminders. To be able to deal with children who have attention disorders, parents must do the following:

1. Seek medical attention for the child so that the parent is aware of what exactly the child is suffering from.

2. The parent should enroll themselves in a support group so that they may receive group counseling from associating with other parents in a similar situation and gain tips and techniques to try with their child.

3. Always give clear instructions, continuous reassurance, and reminders so the child can remain focused for longer. Do not give complicated or ambiguous instructions to a child who has an attention disorder, because they will become easily confused or distracted.

ADHD - Children with Hysteria Crisis

Hysteria is now largely classified as conversion disorder. Hysteria is an outdated term largely used for disorders that have symptoms of a child going blind, being paralyzed, or having hallucinations, which are often accompanied by emotional outbursts. In DSM-5, conversion disorder is placed under the category of Somatic Symptom and Related Disorders, which means that the symptoms and physical pain that a person feels because of the disorder are due to a psychological and not physical cause. Conversion disorder is a "condition in which symptoms and deficits in voluntary motor function suggest a neurological or other physical condition which is in fact not present" (Leary, 2003). Conversion disorder has a prognosis that is very good; research shows that recovery is at 85-97%.

Dealing with a child with conversion disorder is quite difficult, and parents need to employ patience and understanding for what the child says they are experiencing. There is no use shouting at the child and making them feel as if they are not telling the truth about their own bodies. Parents should not make the child feel bad for expressing how they feel or pointing out where they are feeling pain. If a child has ADHD and conversion disorder, it may be difficult for them to even articulate in the first place what symptoms they are experiencing. The following are some tips and techniques that parents should employ in order to deal with a child who has conversion disorder.

Believe the Child

When a child expresses that they can't open their eyes or their legs are not working, for example, it is important for the parents to accept and believe what they say. Whether or not the child's symptoms are fictitious is not for the parent to say. The parent's job is to believe the child and make them feel comfortable enough to express any and everything they may be experiencing. Parents should maintain eye contact and nod their head as their child is speaking, being fully engaged in the conversation and not getting distracted by anything else.

Evaluation

The child should be evaluated by a medical professional, usually by their general practitioner or the pediatrician. Parents cannot assume or diagnose the child at home, as they are not qualified to do so. Additional information about the child's symptoms can be gathered at school so that the parent has a holistic view of what the child has been experiencing. Coupled with the child's behavior and symptoms at home, the parent will then be able to give the pediatrician a complete picture of what the child has been experiencing.

ADHD - Children with Violence Crisis

Rachel was fortunate in that Harvey's outburst was not a violent one, and that he simply cried and screamed with no end in sight. These extreme and intense reactions to certain situations are common among children with ADHD. Unfortunately, not all children react like Harvey. Sometimes, children with ADHD have violent outbursts that occur more frequently than all their other symptoms. It can be a shock when children with ADHD react violently either towards their parents or loved ones, but having a child with ADHD means always being prepared to deal with violent occurrences. A child with ADHD is unable to sufficiently regulate their emotions, and this might result in violence. This is especially true for children who may have co-occurring mood disorders, like depression or anxiety.

There are a variety of things that parents could do to improve their child's anger issues, such as:

1. Enrolling the child in behavioral therapy, such as cognitive behavioral therapy counseling and parent counseling. These kinds of therapy can help children understand that some things aren't necessarily threatening and how to tolerate normal frustrations that come with everyday life. The counseling can also help provide advice and coping mechanisms for both parents and the child (Nigg, 2020).

2. If the child has severe anger issues, then the regular stimulant medication for ADHD may not be as helpful. Parents should consider putting the child on selective serotonin reuptake inhibitors; these medications have been said to reduce irritability and tantrums in children with severe violent symptoms.

3. Exercise can be a constructive and positive release for excess energy and frustration. This can be a channel that the child uses to focus and release all the pent-up aggression so that it is not released in an inappropriate setting. Exercise can have the effect of releasing pressure in regular intervals to prevent that one big explosion.

CHAPTER 7

ADVICE FOR PARENTS

Rachel had never considered that she would be in a position where she had to dedicate her life not only to Harvey, but to understanding what ADHD is. It wasn't something that was second nature to Rachel; she had to learn what was wrong with Harvey, as well as how to deal with the symptoms he exhibited. For Rachel, it was about the sacrifice she had to make for her son to be okay. Of course, not every parent can dedicate themselves in such a big way, but it doesn't make them any less of a good parent than Rachel. However, it is unlikely that a parent who has a child with ADHD will naturally know how to pivot from parenting a child who has no disorders to parenting a child with ADHD.

It takes hard work. It takes commitment. It takes immense drive to learn your child and their symptoms to be able to be a better parent to them. The parent needs to be in tune with how their child is feeling. The world is all about escapes; we escape via technology and other frivolous distractions. However, you cannot run away from or escape ADHD. It has to be faced head on and without fear. A parent who shows bravery in the face of adversity will inspire a frustrated and confused child to face the disorder that may be tormenting them. To cope with the challenges that come with raising a child who has ADHD, there are certain nuggets of wisdom Rachel wishes she had been told.

Accepting ADHD

Accepting plays a large role in taking steps towards dealing with ADHD. Parents have to let go of the urge to want to think that nothing is wrong with their child. ADHD is not a failure for the parents or the child who is diagnosed with it, and since the exact cause of ADHD is unknown, parents should refrain from blaming themselves or wondering what they could have done to prevent it. The parents of the child should divorce the what if's that plague their minds once a diagnosis has been given. If it helps, a parent should grieve the idea of the perfect child. Only after accepting ADHD can a parent provide solutions and support for their child.

Parents may feel shame and disappointment that their child has ADHD. There is no parent who envisions themselves with a child who has special needs, yet every parent considers it as a possibility. No one ever thinks it will be them. There is no use crying over spilled milk, however. If the child is diagnosed with ADHD, then the parent must take a diagnosis in stride and run with it. The diagnosis only means the child's mind functions differently; it doesn't mean that the child is any less capable than their peers. Embracing the disorder means embracing the actual child as they are, not an imaginary, ideal child that was conjured up in fantasies while the mother was still pregnant.

Accepting ADHD may also mean giving that child more attention than a significant other or other children. There are a host of challenges and problems that come along with this disorder, so parents must be flexible with what may come. Only through trial and error will the parent become more comfortable with what ADHD means to them, their family, and the child who was diagnosed. Acceptance is a hard journey, but it is a necessary step in order to move forward to treatment, medication, and therapy. ADHD is not an unconquerable monster, as plenty of parents and children have overcome it and learnt to manage it. This first step opens the mind to not only how things are, but also the potential solutions that could be. It is the biggest hurdle, but once it is overcome, anything is possible.

Don't Let ADHD Win

ADHD can be a consuming disorder in that it turns the affected family's life upside-down. Nothing is ever the same after an ADHD diagnosis; parents will have to adjust their parenting, and the other children will have to accept that the child with the disorder will get more attention than them. The important thing is not to get overwhelmed. Feeling consumed by frustration may cause the parent to lash out at the child. ADHD cannot be seen on the outside, but it is a disability, so parents should employ the same kind of patience and compassion they would with a child with a physical ailment. The child can never divorce themselves from this disability, so if the parent feels angry, they should take a step back to cool off and avoid taking it out on the child.

ADHD is a challenge in this regard, and it will be difficult for parents to stay in the right mindset. Negative thoughts can bombard the mind and leave the parent in a bad space that will prohibit them from providing the necessary support to their child. One bad day can lead into a spiral of several bad days, which is why it is important to nip negativity in the bud before it affects the child. ADHD already causes feelings of frustration and confusion in the child, and they don't need the added negativity from their parents. It sounds easier than what it really is, but it can be achieved. The parent should take it one day at a time and evaluate each day as it comes. Bad days don't last forever.

Under no circumstances can ADHD be allowed to win. The parent must always remember that they are in control. They are the ones who set the boundaries and decide the rules. Parents are the ones who decide acceptable behavior in the home, and what will and will not be allowed from the child, whether or not they have ADHD. The child's symptoms and behaviors can be intimidating and scary, but the parents must remember that they are in control. They should not be intimidated or bullied by outbursts or hysterics. The disorder should not be allowed to take over, and parents should not allow bad behavior just because the child has ADHD.

Coordination of Parental Efforts

The only way that parents can overcome ADHD successfully is if they coordinate their parenting efforts. Children who have ADHD require consistency and stability, which cannot be achieved if the parents are not on the same page. Rachel was able to achieve this with Harvey because Mike had her back; he supported his wife's need to dedicate herself to educating herself about the disorder so as to improve Harvey's quality of life. As an emotional support system, Mike understood his role and what he needed to do for his family to thrive.

All parental figures need to be on the same page. Parental figures do not only include mom and dad, but also grandparents or aunts and uncles who provide primary care to the child. There should be no difference between the mother and the father's parenting when it comes to dealing with a child who has ADHD. Even if the parents are divorced or separated, they need to have the same rules at each of their homes so everything remains stable for the child. If the parents cannot come to an agreement with regard to coordinating their parental efforts, then this will negatively affect the child.

Both parents must be actively involved in all doctor's appointments and therapy sessions relating to the child. If there are any group therapy sessions to attend, then both parents must be in attendance and participate. All the rules and boundaries set for the child must be fully discussed among both parents. Nothing should be left ambiguous. If parents need to, they should write down what they have agreed to do with regard to raising their child and how they will deal with the child's ADHD symptoms. Consulting the child's pediatrician or psychiatrist may also help the parents come to a consensus on how they will deal with the child's disorder.

Supporting Teachers

A teacher most likely would have already identified symptoms in a child who is suspected to have ADHD, because they spend the most time with the child during the day. Unfortunately, teachers may not have special needs training, or the school may not have a special needs class. The child will still need to be in the classroom and learn, so what will that look like? In keeping things consistent for a child who has been diagnosed with ADHD, the parents should also help the child's teachers understand the child's symptoms and ADHD experience. From there, they should share with the teacher different ways to set rules and boundaries, as well as how to discipline the child. The school environment is unique in that the teacher has a number of children that they have to pay attention to. They may not be able to give the child their undivided attention, but they should know how to drive the child to do better.

Communication

Parents need to sit down with the teacher and explain what is important to them with regard to the child. Priorities should be shared so that the teacher doesn't assume what is important to the parent. Grades are not always the only thing that matters; sometimes, all a parent wants is for the child to improve their behavior or social interaction with others. Getting a child with ADHD to sit down and learn the process of starting and finishing their schoolwork is something that may be more of a priority than them being a top student.

Accept Criticism

When a teacher criticizes a child because they can't get their work done, it may feel like a personal attack on the parents. Assessment of the child is part and parcel of their education, and parents should not feel like they are being attacked when they receive these criticisms. Teachers are just highlighting where the problem areas are, and parents should not feel like they're failing in any capacity. The teachers should be assured that the child is a work in progress, and that the parents are doing everything they can to support the child's learning journey. When criticisms are given, the parents should assess honestly and try to offer solutions. The child is special, so the solutions may not be traditional. There is no quick fix when it comes to ADHD, and parents should communicate that to the teachers.

Show Gratitude

If the child is not advancing as the parents expect or thriving in the school environment, the frustration may cause parents to express anger or blame toward the child's teachers. However, playing the blame game takes things backward and offers no progress or solutions. This may also discourage the teacher from putting in the extra effort that is needed for the child to thrive. Instead of showing anger and frustration when the child's ADHD is still standing in the way of their learning, show gratitude for what the teacher has achieved. Parents should tell the teachers every time they notice a positive change or advancement in the child that can be directly attributed to the teacher. Gratitude and appreciation will serve as motivation for the teacher to continue helping the child.

Skills a Parent Must Have to Manage a Child with ADHD

Leadership

Parenting a child with ADHD means certain skills must be mastered in order for the child to succeed at managing their disorder. One of these skills is leadership. A parent must coordinate a small team of professionals or people who will aid in supporting the child. For example, the parent will have to cooperate with the child's doctor and see what treatments or medications need to be taken by the child and ensure they complete everything prescribed to them. Further, these treatments need to be communicated to family members and caregivers so that the child is receiving adequate care. The parent must also transform everyone's mindset and how they view ADHD and the child who has it, which will help them stop being intimidated by the disorder and motivate them to overcome it.

Advocacy

Parents must be prepared to fight for their child. Fighting in this sense is not physical; the parents should know the rights of the ADHD child and what can be done to better their condition. For example, if the state pays for their medication, then the parent should make sure that it is given free of charge. If there's certain legislation about the child's rights with regard to their education, then the parent should know those laws and advocate for them at the child's school. The parent must be knowledgeable and educated about what ADHD means legally for the child, as they won't be able to protect the rights of that child otherwise. The parents should learn about the legal system and how to apply laws to their situation; if need be, they should hire an attorney to assist in advocating for their child's rights.

Discipline

It takes extra effort to coordinate the life of a child with ADHD. If parents are to lessen the effect that the symptoms have on the child's life, then they need to enact long-lasting changes in the child's life. To ensure consistency, the parents of the child must be very disciplined. Every day, the same rules must be applied without any deviation. The road to effective parenting of a child with ADHD is long and challenging, there are no shortcuts. Parents cannot let petty squabbles amongst themselves or with other professionals derail from the goal of simplifying the life of their child. Focusing on the child and making their lives easier should be the parent's top priority at all times.

Problem-solving

It wouldn't make sense if the parents of the child with ADHD didn't have problem-solving skills. There will be numerous instances where the child's disorder will present in such a way that the entire family will be disrupted by it. The parents will need to figure out how to parent creatively while also giving the other children, or their spouse, attention. Creative problem-solving will keep everyone happy, while also keeping the child happy and meeting their needs. Problem-solving will require thinking outside the box and pushing the limits of the imagination. Solving the issues that may arise due to ADHD is going to push the parents of the child away from traditional disciplinary methods and propel them into uncharted territory, but the parents should adopt a can-do attitude and do the best they can.

Common Mistakes

Using ADHD to Make the Child Feel Bad About Themselves

Although the child is different and the disorder makes it difficult for them to do normal things like finishing a task or sitting still, it is not the child's fault that they are built that way. Making the child feel bad about their disorder when they have no control over it is not acceptable, and parents should never weaponize ADHD. The child may already be feeling stressed, confused, or frustrated, and making them feel bad or guilty about themselves is not conducive to progress.

Losing Control

The symptoms of ADHD mean the child may lose control of their temper and begin an endless loop of hysterical cries, kicking, screaming, and violent outbursts. A child with ADHD will mature only after the age 25, so the only person who can exercise self-control is the parent or caregiver. However, it is hard not to get angry or upset if someone is kicking and screaming or beating you with their fists. The difference between the child and the parent is that the parent is able to control themselves. Self-control will ensure the parents actions are not fueled by anger. The parent should never lose their temper in the presence of the child, and they should not be controlled by frustration and anger. Being agitated only adds fuel to the fire and will further escalate a tense situation.

Thinking You Can Relate

Unless you are an adult who has ADHD, it is impossible to truly understand what the child who has the disorder is going through. Sympathizing is not the same as relatability, and parents will often feel as if they understand when they have no idea what it is like. Only those with ADHD will know what it means to have the disorder. It is a mistake for one to think they know what ADHD is like when they have never had it, and this is where most parents go wrong. These parents need to accept that they have no idea what it is like to have ADHD and let the child try to express how and what they feel. When a parent thinks they understand what ADHD is, they can project expectations onto the child and create situations that are ripe for disappointment. If a person doesn't have ADHD, they can get an idea of the disorder through extensive education, but they will never truly understand what it is like to have it.

Excluding the Child in Planning

When it comes to decision-making concerning a child who has special needs, there are usually three key individuals involved: the child's parents, the child's doctor, and the child's educators. These individuals will communicate and plan a way forward to make the child's life easier and to assist in their development so that they are not left behind. Oftentimes, this is done without the child's participation. Adults often think that they know better and what will be best for the child. Unfortunately, excluding the child in planning how their life should be may result in even more frustration in the lives of both the child and the parents. Allowing the child to be a part of the conversation and the planning of their lives could provide key insights that adults overlook, and also creates a camaraderie and an overall feeling that "we are in this together". In the future, the child will not be afraid to go to their parents with tweaks and suggestions to their schedule or routine. The child will also see the value of their opinion and feel more in control of their life.

Not Having the Same Rules

A child with ADHD may seem chaotic and unhinged. Their creative nature may discourage parents from committing them to a routine or schedule. For children with ADHD to thrive, they need structure and predictability. Wherever they go, their rules should remain the same. Whether they are at grandma's house or at their father's house, their punishments and behavioral plan should be identical. All the parental figures must agree on what rules should apply and stick to them. The consistency and predictability will allow the child to thrive, reducing the effect that the symptoms of ADHD have on their everyday life.

Expecting Immediate Results

Once the child is diagnosed and is either prescribed medication or a behavioral plan, improvements do not happen overnight. It takes some months, or even a few years, to see the true results of what the child was prescribed. Even if the parents stick to a rigid behavioral plan, there's no guarantee that they will see results anytime soon. Slow progress means that parents should not only focus on the overall result, but also on the small wins along the way. The parents should let the child know that they see their efforts and that they are pleasing. The parents should encourage the child by letting them know that although they are not at the final goal yet, they are well on their way as they have had all these other small wins, and that these will add up and make that big win that they are looking for. Managing ADHD is definitely a marathon, so be sure to keep your child motivated.

Disclosing the Disorder to Others

There are certain people that need to know of the child's ADHD diagnosis, including the child's medical practitioners, teachers, and other adult caregivers. In cases where the child has siblings and they are at the age where they can understand, then it is also important to disclose to the child siblings that the child has ADHD. Outside of the above mentioned, it is not necessary to freely disclose your child's Neurodevelopmental disorder. The disorder affects the child, and they should be the ones to disclose their disorder should they feel comfortable enough to. A common mistake parents make is to freely announce that their child has ADHD without consulting the child. ADHD is not a quirk or a personality trait, therefore it should not be talked about without considering the child's right to privacy. Parents can potentially consult the child to see if they are comfortable with disclosing that they have ADHD.

Believing Information on the Internet Without Verifying the

Source

There are multiple articles on the Internet that have to do with ADHD. The first thing that most parents will do once they receive the news that their child has ADHD is to Google what the disorder is and how to help their child. There is nothing wrong with doing this, but parents must make sure that the information they use will be beneficial to their child and how they are presenting. If the article is about a child who is showing a hyperactive/impulsive presentation of ADHD, the information will not assist a child who is exhibiting a combined or inattentive presentation of ADHD. Some articles are written by journalists who gather information from various sources, and therefore should not carry the same weight as an article from a medical journal. The parents should be able to decipher between articles that have weight and those that do not.

CHAPTER 8

HELPFUL TOOLS FOR ACTION

Children who can Rationalize, Identify, and Communicate Their Concerns

Explaining what is going on in the mind of a child with ADHD is important to help the parents understand their psyche. Without this information, parents will not understand the frustrations the child has to deal with on a daily basis. Explaining the types of symptoms the child may present will also help the parents prepare themselves for what is to come. The presentation of a child's ADHD symptoms may change over time, so sensitizing a parent on what could happen equips them with the knowledge necessary to cope. All this information is helpful, but it is not enough to help a parent deal with a child with ADHD. Rachel needed more than just knowledge in order to properly alleviate Harvey's ADHD symptoms. She knew it would take more than just reading about the disorder, but what else could she do?

There is no cure for ADHD, but there are certain techniques and methods that the child's parents can employ in order to properly address the disorder and effectively parent a child who can rationalize and communicate their concerns. Fortunately, a child like this can fully articulate how they feel and what they like and don't like. They become a guiding factor of what works and what does not work if parents include them in their treatment plans. Below will be a practical guide on how to handle a child who has ADHD, how to speak to them, and other techniques and tips to practically apply at home. The theory behind ADHD has been left in previous chapters, and now we will be delving into the application of certain skills to deal with ADHD in children.

Practical Strategies and Tools for ADHD

Education

Aside from the outlined ADHD symptoms as per DSM-5, there are co-occurring disorders that may also develop alongside ADHD. When a parent is well-educated on what those are, then they can spot them when the symptoms arise. Co-occurring disorders include, but are not limited to: depression, anxiety, learning disorders, conduct disorders, and oppositional defiant disorder. The parents of the child could also benefit from taking a behavioral parent training class, which is said to provide age-appropriate positive reinforcement techniques that leave parents feeling less stressed and experiencing fewer problems with their child's ADHD.

Positive Attention

Set aside personal one-on-one time with your child to bond and play with them in a relaxed environment. The time should not be an excessive amount like three hours, because children with ADHD can lose focus quite easily. Even as little as 15 minutes can be effective. There should be no interruptions or distractions. Children with ADHD can feel like they only get attention when they are bad and seek to carry on bad behavior to get the attention of their parents. This enjoyable time will reinforce the feelings of safety and stability, while also easing the child's anxiety and any feelings of uncertainty. This will assist in easing the attention-seeking tendencies that tend to accompany the symptoms of a child with ADHD. With this positive attention, the parent seeks to show the child that they are an important part of their life and that they are loved and cared for.

Use Time-outs

A time-out can be used to help ease frustrations when the child is overwhelmed. Traditionally, time-outs are used for punishments when the child has been bad. However, the delayed mental development and maturing of a child with ADHD causes confusion and inability to process information as effectively as their peers, meaning they can easily feel overwhelmed with everything that goes on in daily life and may need a moment to escape it all. Time-outs can be used to help a child calm down their body and their thoughts. A quiet space in the home with comfortable seating should be set aside as the space for time-outs. During episodes of frustration, the parent should calmly guide the child towards that area so that they quiet their minds. When done often enough, the child will automatically go to that space when they are feeling overwhelmed or wanting to lash out and actually prevent a possible meltdown or outburst.

Manage Time
Children with ADHD have no perception of time. Set timers when doing tasks, so when the alarm goes off, the child will know it is time to do the next task. Set alarms for when it's time to wake up and take medication, or for when it is time to leave the house and go to school. This will provide a structured tracking of time.

Create a Reward System
A reward system can be used as positive reinforcement. The reward system should be designed in such a way that the child can work towards rewards they like in a short amount of time. The rewards could include electronics time, ice cream, or anything else they may enjoy as a treat. Good behavior such as putting toys away, sitting still for an entire meal, or finishing homework of their own volition could earn them tokens or marks toward their reward. Different amounts of tokens for different rewards would motivate the child more; for example, a trip to the toy store would require more good behavior (tokens) from the child than getting served a dessert of their choice. The system can be designed however the parent wishes.

How to Talk to a Child with ADHD

Give Specific Instructions

Children with ADHD do not do well with ambiguity; they will not benefit from an instruction like "clean the house". If you want the child to understand what you are saying, then you need to speak in a more effective manner. Instead of using the ambiguous "clean the house", issue out more specific instructions like "mop the floors" and "load the dishwasher", as those instructions guide to what specifically needs to be done.

Praise Your Child for Every Good Deed

Children with ADHD are accustomed to being chastised, as they were likely considered 'bad children' before they were diagnosed with ADHD. These children are not accustomed to receiving praise, yet it can be used as a powerful positive reinforcement tool. If the child does something good, praise them for it. This recognition of good will motivate the child to do more good things or behave in a good way so they can receive more praise. The parent must use praises like "well done", "you did so well", and "you must be so proud of yourself" to praise the child on what they have done right.

Speak Calmly

Children with ADHD are more likely to spiral into tantrums and outbursts. This will result in screaming matches and hysterical crying. In the face of this, no matter how agitated the parent is, they should never mimic the behavior of the child or lash out. No matter how unhinged the child gets, the parent should always remain calm and speak to the child in a soothing manner. This tone will disarm the child and show them that their behavior will not move the parent. The consistent soothing tone of the parent will show the child that they have a consistent calm force amidst the chaos in their life. It will further show that the parent is not susceptible to manipulation; no matter how bad the lashing out gets, the parent is not swayed by it and will remain firm in their guidance and disciplining of the child.

How to Discipline a Child with ADHD

Communicate What They Did Wrong
Sometimes, parents are so focused on being disapproving or dishing out punishments that they don't communicate what the child did wrong well enough. ADHD children may even face a spanking when all they need to experience is being told where they went wrong. If the parent continuously points out what the child is doing wrong, the child will start to notice their bad behavior after the third or fourth time. They can then start to notice when they are going wrong, and perhaps even try to stop themselves when they notice they are going down the wrong path. Use specific language. It will not help to ambiguously tell your child "don't do that", so give specific feedback like "stop banging your head on the table" or "stop shouting in the house".

Follow Through on Punishment
The parents of a child who has ADHD might feel bad dishing out punishment, but it is part and parcel of everyone's childhood. The saying "spare the rod, spoil the child" applies here in a metaphorical sense. There are behaviors that your child can't control, but they are also behaviors that they can; good manners is something a child with ADHD can learn just like a child without it. Good behavior and manners are learned by correcting bad behavior, and punishment is one of the ways a parent can correct bad behavior. If a parent doesn't follow through on dealing with bad behavior, the child will learn that the parent is all bark and no bite. Following through on punishments, no matter how unpleasant, will show the child that the parent means business and should be listened to.

Explain What is Happening

The child should understand what is happening during every step of the way. When they are behaving badly, they should be warned no more than three times. They should then be told what the consequences of their actions are and what that will mean for them. For example, if a child is told to sit and finish their snack and they fail to do so, they should be asked to sit and finish their snack three times. If they fail to do so, the parent should explain that because they failed to sit and finish their snack, they will not be getting an ice pop as a treat. If the child protests, explain that they will have an opportunity to earn the ice pop if they sit and finish their snack next time. Communication is key, since it lets their brain attempt to connect the dots and understand what is happening when it happens to eliminate confusion.

How to Recognize and Prevent Explosive Anger

Assess Sensitivity

Every parent knows what their child is more likely to be susceptible to. ADHD causes emotional dysregulation, which means the child is more likely to cry easily or experience feelings of intense anger. The children that show this type of sensitivity will have a higher chance of displaying explosive anger. The parent should assess how sensitive the child is and if their emotional reactions are appropriate. The emotional reactions that parents should look out for are the child being easily saddened, angered, irritated, and frustrated.

Establish Patterns

If parents observe their child closely, they may be able to see patterns emerging. For example, they may become more agitated or irritable right before or after going to school. There will be a particular time in the day when your child's anger seems to peak, possibly due to anxiety or frustration. Knowing when these episodes of peaked anger occur can help parents predict and prepare, helping to defuse the child before their anger explodes. The anger of a child with ADHD may become more intense when they get home from school, when they're feeling tired, fatigued, or hungry, or when they're just experiencing frustration with a task. Medication wearing off may also create a ripe situation for anger. The key is to anticipate these episodes.

How to Deal with Explosive Anger in a Child with ADHD

Remain Calm

Witnessing a child become consumed with anger can rouse different types of emotions in a parent. For Rachel, she felt helpless and unprepared to deal with Harvey's outbursts, and they weren't even characterized by anger. How will a parent faced with the ugliness of their child's anger react? The only way to respond is to remain calm. The child may spew unspeakable language toward their parents, but they must remain calm throughout the anger episode. Do not mimic the child's anger or frustrations. Remember they don't mean anything they do or say. It may feel like a personal attack, but the child does not know better for them to act better. Remain calm no matter what.

Let the Explosive Anger Happen

Unless the child is hurting themselves or others, let them explode. If the child is crying or screaming, let them get it all out for a few minutes before attempts are made to calm them down. Sometimes, the child has pent-up aggression and the only way to release that is to let the explosion happen. That way, everyone can begin on a new slate and begin to piece the pieces together of how they got there. From there, an assessment of why the explosion happened can be made, and the child can be given better coping mechanisms to aid in dealing with their daily frustrations.

Don't Blame, Comfort

When the child has an explosive anger episode, the parent needs to be there to comfort the child when they are having the outburst. It is not helpful to say things like "But you should have known" or "It's your own fault". The child is not in control of their executive functions, and they cannot foresee that they will get overwhelmed to the point of explosion. It is not their fault. When a child with ADHD explodes with anger, comfort them and assure them that you are there to make their life better. It is tempting to try to turn the explosion into a teaching moment, but now is not the time, as the child is coming down from an intense emotional reaction. Comfort them at times during explosions, and dont put blame on them. Blame increases anxiety and guilt and confusion, which is not what they need.

How to Plan and Prepare for the Explosion

Prepare a Safe Place

Prepare a small space in the house that will have a calming effect on the child. The color blue is a calming color, but the space can easily be painted the child's favorite color if that is what works better. Fill the place with cushions and soft textures so that the child is surrounded by that plush, comfortable feeling. For example, consider the use of bean bags rather than chairs. A water feature can bring a calming effect to any room, and there are portable small fountains that can be placed in the room to create a zen zone. This place can be where the child goes after their explosion ends to reset their mind. Posters can be placed on the walls as well to soothe the child, and the space can even be outside in the garden.

Figure Out What Calms the Child

Every child is different, and what calms one may not calm another. This will be a trial-and-error journey on the part of the parent with them trying to figure out what calms their child. One child will respond well to hugs and being held while they cry, while another may prefer not to be touched and to be left alone while they lie on a plush carpet listening to calming music. Find out what calms the child and keep exploring. Find more than one thing so you can create a diverse way to calm your child. If you use one method for too long, it may lose its effectiveness.

Create an Action Plan

Once you have discovered what calms your child, you can create an action plan of what to do when they have an outburst. Your partner or the members of the household should memorize this plan and know what steps to take and the order in which to take them. It must be clear and simple to follow so that everyone can be involved in helping the child to calm down. Involve the child and see what their input is in their action plan. Once it has been formulated, it is important to always follow it, because it will create a sense of security for the child when they are in need.

How to Problem-solve Collaboratively with a Child with ADHD

The problems that come with ADHD forces families to work together to lessen the burden. Teamwork and cooperation from each member of the family, including the child who has ADHD, may ease the transition into a new life with a different set of rules for one or more family members. If a parent is not involved in actively using the child's ADHD symptoms, then the child will not prosper. If the parent makes all the decisions without consulting the child and other family members, then the child will not prosper. Only when there is a mix of active collaborative cooperation can ADHD be addressed effectively.

Collaborative problem-solving educates adults on various strategies to help children who have been diagnosed with ADHD. This type of problem-solving doesn't treat the symptoms, but it works to help parents identify triggers that may lead to problematic behavior. Collaborative problem-solving is more about prevention than a cure, especially because there is no cure for ADHD. Using this method, parents are encouraged not to wait until bad behavior manifests, but instead to try to anticipate the triggers. The parent must be proactive to assist the child in avoiding the place where the symptoms take over. The idea is to lessen the likelihood of undesirable outcomes (Howes, n.d.).

Both the adult and the child will be equipped with skills that will reduce anger and frustration so that they will be able to adapt, cope, and deal with difficult situations. In this way, the parent will be able to effectively alert the child to what could happen and guide them towards a better solution that reduces the child's confusion and frustration. This will also condition the child on how to better respond to situations they deem intimidating (Howes, n.d.).

Children who Cannot Rationalize, Identify, and Communicate Their Concerns

Physical and Mental Attitudes to Adopt

1. Patience must be exercised when trying to communicate with a child who is not able to. Let the child try to communicate with you, and if they are unable, suggest to them what you may think is wrong and allow them to agree or disagree.

2. Be positive. Do not be discouraged by setbacks that occur due to the difficult nature of parenting a child who is unable to articulate what is wrong; soldier on.

3. Be consistent in carrying out the action plan for the treatment of the child. Stick to every schedule made, as well as any behavioral plans.

How to Recognize and Prevent Explosive Anger

A child who cannot properly articulate what they're feeling or what they're frustrated about may exhibit their anger in various non-verbal ways. Their anger outbursts may be a little different from a child who can articulate, scream, and shout about why they are angry. If my child cannot rationalize their concerns, they may experience a higher level of frustration and confusion. To prevent explosive anger, the parent must always ask a child if they are okay. Using simple language like "happy" or "sad" to ask the child how they are feeling will help to find out where they are mentally. Having an idea of where the child is emotionally at every turn will assist in preventing an emotional breakdown, because the parent will have a chance to catch the child before they descend into a downward emotional spiral.

It is important to recognize the signs of explosive anger in the child as it is about to happen. Notice the child's facial expressions and if they have their face in a scowl. Examine their body language and if they have an open stance, or if their hands are crossed and their fists are clenched. Look to see if their jaw is clenched or if they're stomping their feet. Body language will tell you what you need to know about the mood of the child and allow you to predict if an emotional outburst is coming. Knowing particulars about the child's daily life in the home and at school will also help give insights about future upsetting moments that could trigger explosive anger.

How to Manage the Child's Explosive Anger

Strategies covered in the above sections on how to deal with explosive anger regarding children that are able to rationalize, identify, and communicate their concerns are still applicable here. When a child is experiencing explosive anger, it is important to remain calm, let them get all of the negative emotions out, and then provide comfort to them. Managing and dealing with explosive anger in a child with ADHD is no small feat, and a person must be mentally prepared to provide a lot of emotional support to the child.

How to Understand the Child's Learning Processes

Learning styles are not the same from one person to the other. One person may prefer to learn via visual material, while another person would prefer to learn by hearing lectures being taught to them. The brain of an ADHD child is not the same as the brain of a child without the disorder. Teaching a child who has ADHD in a style they prefer may actually allow them to focus better and retain more information. If educational lessons are tailored to the needs and preferences of a child with ADHD, they will reap the benefits.

They are different types of learning styles that can be applied in order to deliver information. From these styles emerged different types of learners, who prefer specific mediums of learning that engage their minds better than traditional learning. Visual learners are those who prefer to learn using their sight and do better when there are colorful diagrams, educational videos, charts, or activity on the whiteboard. When visual learners see information, it makes it easier for them to absorb it and retain it for longer. An auditory learner, on the other hand, is one who is able to retain more information if it is delivered orally and they get the opportunity to hear it. These types of students benefit from recorded lectures or reading course material out loud.

Lastly, you have a kinesthetic learner, who wants to be fully emerged in the learning process by being fully emerged in hands-on activities that aid in absorption of information. These kinds of students are often viewed as fidgety or unable to sit still, when they actually just want to be physically involved in the lesson. Kinesthetic learners benefit the most from field trips, science experiments, building models, and art and crafts. Finding out the best method of learning for the child will maximize their learning potential.

After understanding the child's learning style and process, it is beneficial to share that with their educators so that they can integrate that in the child's daily lessons. Regardless of the child's learning style, it is important for a child with ADHD to always sit in the front so they do not get lost in the lessons. The educator will have the ability to make sure they stay in the loop if they are sitting at the front or close to the front.

How to Understand a Child's Emotional Processes

The inability for a child with ADHD to regulate their emotions means that they are prone to haphazard emotional episodes. They may struggle with completing normal tasks and get carried away with distractions. The child is unable to feel the appropriate emotion at the right intensity, meaning their daily life can be a struggle to get through. Manifestations of this inability to control emotions show up in the child sharing too much information, not being able to look at the bigger picture, losing perspective, saying things that they later regret, anger outbursts, and behaving spontaneously.

It should be understood that the child can get carried away with emotions that they are currently feeling and may act on that temporary emotion without thinking about the consequences, or how the impulsive action will affect them or others. This can make the child's moods seem as if they are sporadic and unstable. The parent of the child should always take into consideration that the child has no control over what they feel, how they feel it, and for how long they feed it. If they understand this, they will be able to understand the child and lead them from a place of compassion and patience.

CHAPTER 9

WHAT WE CAN TEACH OUR CHILDREN

It is not enough for parents to have coping tools and skills, as we must equip the children with coping skills as well. The parents of a child with ADHD will not always be next to that child; at some point, the parent has to let the child out into the world and hope they have done enough to prepare them for what is in the world. Parents can only go so far in assisting the child, but the truth is that the child has to be equipped with knowledge so that they can manage their own disorder.

ADHD is not a dirty little secret, and the child should be thoroughly educated about it as well as how to prevent and cope with symptoms. They need to be given the opportunity to learn about themselves and their own presentations of ADHD. Only with this knowledge will the child begin to prosper and become skilled at preventing outbursts and meltdowns. Managing their symptoms will also allow them to build confidence in their ability to regulate themselves and their emotions.

It is a long road, especially because the child may find it hard to focus on what you are teaching them. Take time to teach them the same skills each and every day so that it becomes a part of their routine. Practice makes perfect. It is also not just about the end goal, but also the journey. Parents must encourage the child at every turn and show them that it is okay to mess up and not get it right the first time. The child will discover a lot about themselves as they go, and it will reveal their weaknesses as well as their strengths. Both should be celebrated.

Before anything else is considered, the doctor may want to enroll the child in behavioral therapy and prescribe medication as the first line of defense against ADHD once the child has been diagnosed. This is what happens in the normal course of treatment. There are alternative methods of treatment or coping skills that the child can be taught to supplement the prescribed treatment. Variety is the spice of life, and a child with ADHD has a variety of coping mechanisms that can help manage their symptoms.

Coping Strategies for Children

Get a Pet

In order to help a child ease the frustration that comes with ADHD, they could be given a pet like a cat or a dog. A pet will teach a child responsibility and empathy, as the child will know that they have to take care of their pet everyday. When the child is walking the dog or playing with it in the yard, they are using up any excess energy they have. Children with ADHD, especially those who present as hyperactive or impulsive, will have a lot of fun playing with a pet as they'll have a healthy outlet for all the energy they seem to have. The anxiety and confusion children with ADHD often experience can be quelled by petting the animal and cuddling with it.

Research shows that people who have trauma or PTSD can benefit from having an animal companion to soothe their anxiety. Getting a child a pet could provide comfort for them during times where they feel like the world does not understand them, and having an animal companion may provide uncomplicated companionship. People have a hard time relating to and understanding a child with ADHD, including their peers, meaning it may be hard for them to make friends to begin with. This pet will be their confidante and make their life a little less solitary. The child will be able to rely on the pet during times of frustration and anger.

Rhythmic Movements

Research shows that rhythmic motions, such as the motions of a rocking chair or a swing, can be soothing for a child with ADHD. Other rhythmic movements to assist a child when they are having trouble focusing due to too much excitement or tiredness include throwing a ball back and forth, climbing stairs, or marching in one spot. These types of rhythmic activities provide a sensory input that balances the child when they are feeling off-balance. What exactly are rhythmic movements, and how can we teach them to children with ADHD in order to help them cope with their symptoms?

Rhythmic movements are repetitive gentle rocking motions that include reflex integration. Research states that they open the mind and stimulate pathways in the brain in order to aid in learning, ease of movement, and achieving emotional balance (About RMTi - Rhythmic Movement, n.d.). The benefits for the child with ADHD are obvious because they have trouble focusing, regulating emotions, and learning delays. There are organizations like Rhythmic Movement Training International who make it their mission to provide rhythmic movement therapy as a service.

A child can be provided with a swing (that doesn't spin), a rocking chair, or a ball to throw against a wall so that they are able to do these rhythmic movements when they feel off-balance. If it seems that the child is getting flustered or frustrated, they can be reminded to do any of the rhythmic movements that they have been guided through. There will be an immense difference in a few weeks after introducing the child to these motions. They can resort to them on their own in time.

Therapy (ADHD Coaching)

Children can be helped to cope with their ADHD by getting an ADHD coach. This coach can be found via the ADHD Coaches Organization (ACO). The purpose of the coach is to use various methods to help the child take control of their lives and develop necessary skills to navigate daily life helping to impart the skills that people without the conditions take for granted onto them. This type of therapy allows the coach to work with the child realistically to develop social, mental, and emotional skills in order to navigate their own emotions better.

The coach will teach the child how to do the following:

1. Develop and maintain social relationships.

2. Time management.

3. Effective communication.

4. Living a healthy, balanced life.

5. Assessing and making informed choices.

The skills the coach will teach also include space and task management, living an organized life, and following through on what they are supposed to do. This can also include financial and career development once the child is of age.

Unfortunately, there is a cost to ADHD coaching, much like life coaching or sessions with a therapist. These sessions can cost up to $250 or more for one hour, and the parents might not always have those kinds of funds for ADHD coaching. The costs can negatively impact the family or cause the child to miss out on this type of therapy altogether.

Strategies to Improve the Child's Attention Span

The attention span of a child differs according to age. Children who are three years old can pay attention for around six to nine minutes, whereas a child who is four years old can pay attention for up to 12 minutes. Five-year-olds have an impressive attention span of up to 15 minutes. Logically, a child who is three years old will have a shorter attention span than a child who is nine or 10 years old. Parents should notice it increasing with age. When a child is younger, they sit and concentrate for shorter periods of time like screen time or snack time, whereas an older child can even sit for an hour long exam at school. Either way, they have to be able to spend some time focusing on tasks, as they will need to do so throughout their schooling lives and at home.

One of the things that parents struggle to do is get their child to pay attention long enough to complete a task. This task may include things like eating a meal, doing homework, and cleaning a bedroom. Children who can't pay attention struggle to learn important social lessons, and they may miss out on learning opportunities. It is not enough to scream and shout at your child to try to get them to sit still long enough to do something; in fact, this is discouraged. Due to the fact that the symptoms that a child with ADHD experiences are out of their control, it is also not their fault that they can't concentrate on something for extended periods of time.

If your child is diagnosed later in their childhood, then it becomes more difficult to try to teach them how to concentrate. The earlier you teach your child how to focus or concentrate on one today, the easier it becomes to focus as they get older. If the child is taught later in life, however, it's not a lost cause. The idea behind teaching a child to focus and concentrate is so that they can keep up with their peers and with the rate at which they learn at school, but if the child is struggling, there are certain activities or skills parents can teach to improve the attention span of that child.

It goes without saying that going to sleep for an adequate amount of time and good nutrition will help to boost the child's ability to focus for longer. When a child has had a good night's rest, they are more capable of sitting for longer periods of time to complete a task. If they haven't had enough sleep, they will not be able to concentrate at all, and they may even be irritable. When a child is given good nutrition, they will be able to concentrate better, because their brain develops at the expected rate for a child that age as it receives all necessary nutrients needed for healthy development. A lack of nutrition will stunt the growth of the brain, acting as a hindrance to the mind being able to concentrate.

Play Games

Playing games with your child forces them to concentrate on what is happening, the rules of the game, and whose turn it is next. When the child is playing, they have to focus on what's going on, which trains their minds to concentrate while they are also having fun. Age-appropriate board games like snakes and ladders or Ludo, as well as Simon Says, will keep the child's attention and teach them to zone in on what's happening.

Puzzles or Art

Doing a puzzle or a work of art, such as painting or coloring, gives the child encouragement to focus until completion. This kind of activity has an end result, which helps the child see the project through to the end because there is a payoff that they want to experience after all the hard work they put in. Once completed, the parent can celebrate with the child and praise them for creating a wonderful piece of art. The activity should be age-appropriate and not too intimidating for the child.

For small children, it's better to stick to a puzzle that takes less than 10 minutes to complete or a picture that is not too complicated to color or paint. Activities that are too long might discourage the child and make them feel bad because they are not able to sit and finish them in one sitting. Once your child is able to finish a four-piece puzzle, for example, try to get them to finish a six-piece puzzle. Over time, they will learn to concentrate on longer and bigger puzzles.

Frequent Movement Breaks

If a person works at a job where they are sitting in front of the computer or at a desk for long periods of time, it is easy to lose focus. Boredom comes quickly, and it can become difficult to focus. In the moment when a person gets up to make a cup of tea or to go to the bathroom, the body is reset. When the person gets back to their desks, their mind will be motivated to apply a new focus to what they had been doing before. It is this simple movement task that ensures that the body resumes concentration and finishes what was started.

It is unreasonable for adults to expect children to sit for hours on end without a break, and it is even more unreasonable to expect this of a child who has ADHD and struggles to sit still for a long period of time. We all need a break to refresh when we have been sitting and focusing on a task for a long time. To maximize the amount of time a child with ADHD can focus, give them frequent movement breaks in between tasks or during a task that requires an extended period of time.

Give the child breaks every 20 minutes, and allow them to walk around the room, stretch their limbs, or do 10 quick jumping jacks. The child could also bend forward to touch their toes several times or shake their limbs to and fro. This will be an opportunity to re-energize the body as well as the mind and refresh the child for the activities at hand. If they had been struggling with the activity they were focusing on, a movement break may renew their motivation to try again and complete the task.

Read Bedtime Stories

Reading a bedtime story to the child will require them to use their ears for listening as the story is being told. Their minds have to be engaged and remember what is being said, and their imagination has to put all the pieces together. This activity will stretch the child's imagination capabilities and have them hanging on to every word. As the parent is reading the story, it helps to show the child the pictures that are in the book. To keep the child even more engaged, tell them bedtime stories about topics that they are specifically interested in.

Books to help expand a child's vocabulary and auditory awareness. If it is a book with a moral lesson, it is also teaching the child social skills. Reading is a learning experience, but it is also an opportunity to bond with your child and discover what parts of the story excite the child and which parts have them a little bored. The activity of reading to your child is not visual, so it is wonderful for building their attention span and listening skills. You can also involve their other senses by asking them questions, or by having them point to touch the book as they answer your questions.

Limit Screen Time

Nowadays, a lot of parents rely on technology to raise their child. In the age of the Internet, it is not only the television that parents need to worry about; the children have access to tablets and smartphones, and they may use these to watch YouTube and other streaming services. There is nothing wrong with allowing a child to watch educational programs, cartoons, or playing video games. The problem comes in when the child is experiencing screen time for too long.

Although a child can sit and face the television or computer screen for hours on end, it doesn't mean that they are actually paying attention, as they may be simply passively looking at the screen. The images are said to be flashing at a rate that the brain is not accustomed to. The mind sees this as unnatural, but if it keeps happening, then it becomes used to this hyperstimulation. When the brain is used to this fast and flashy type of stimulation, it disadvantages a child when they are placed in a normal environment.

When the child is expected to interact with others and operate in a normal environment, their brain will struggle because the normal environment stimulates them at a much slower pace and the information will be processed at a natural rate that the child is not used to. This means if the child is behind a screen for far too long, they will not be able to function normally in a classroom, a playground, or at home.

It is advised that screen time for a child with ADHD is limited to up to an hour a day. They are already struggling with focusing and concentration, so extended screen time may further deteriorate what little attention span they have. The child should be encouraged to take part in leisure activities such as puzzles, coloring, playing outside, or doing household chores so that they can function normally in a normal environment.

Strategies to Calm Moments of Impulsivity and Anger

Previous chapters have discussed how to recognize, cope and deal with anger in a child who has ADHD. Chapter 8 specifically deals with practical strategies on how to deal with explosive anger in a child with ADHD, as well as how to plan and prepare for the explosion. Due to that, we will not be focusing on anger, but on impulsiveness. ADHD can present in many ways, and one of those ways is impulsiveness, where a person will act without thinking. This includes interrupting people with their own thoughts or grabbing items while someone else is using them.

Impulsiveness is already an issue in toddlers, as they are unable to wait their turn or understand why they need to wait for someone to finish using a toy they'd like. They want to do as they please at all times without considering or listening to their parents or anyone else. This is a real issue with ADHD, where the child will do a lot of things without thinking them through first. Not being able to control your impulses may lead to impaired decision-making. How can a parent calm the child during moments of impulsiveness and help to ease the symptoms?

Repeat What They Were Told

Children who struggle with impulsiveness most likely didn't hear what they were told to do. If they didn't hear what they were told to do, then they are not going to follow instructions effectively. When giving instructions to a child who has ADHD, always make sure that they repeat what was said to them. Repeating the instructions is a good way to see if the child has fully understood the directives they were given. If the child got the instruction wrong, then it is also a chance for the parent to correct and guide the child in the right direction.

If the child has understood the directions given, they should be allowed to then take action. Nothing should be done if they have not yet grasped what they are being instructed to do. Having them repeat what has been said will keep track of whether or not they have listened. To further make sure that they don't get lost in the communication, always remember to keep the instructions simple. If the directions have multiple steps, make sure that they are written down so that the child has something to refer to if they forget.

Introduce Impulse Control Games

Impulse control games allow a child to practice their self-control in a casual, fun environment. An example of a game that forces you to exercise self-control is Jenga. If the child is not paying attention and is moving too fast, then the delicate tower will come toppling down. Children focusing on playing Jenga have no choice but to slow down and exercise restraint when necessary. Games like musical statue, where students have to dance while music plays and stop dancing while the music stops, and musical chairs will also allow them to learn impulse control.

When a child is playing this game, they are realizing that they don't have to do what they want when they want. It shows them that there are rules and they have to follow them. They get to practice self-control over their bodies and movements, while also having the opportunity to learn and socialize. Parents can play these types of games with all their children and their entire family on a regular basis to see results with impulse control in their child. An important thing to remember is that impulse control can always be learned, even by a child who has ADHD.

Teach Calming Tools

When a child is unable to control her impulses or is feeling angry, it is important for them to know how to calm themselves down, as their parents may not be there to calm them down in every situation. For example, when a child is at school, the parents will be nowhere near the situations they get themselves in on the playground or in the classroom, and teachers will not always be there to break up fights or displays of intense emotions. A child with ADHD who is presenting with impulsiveness must know how to calm those feelings by themselves.

The parents of the child must equip the child with skills that will aid them in calming their intense feelings, and they should be taught how to reboot their system and get back to a state of calmness. Deep breathing exercises may be used in order to ease frustration and reduce impulsive outbursts. To begin the deep breathing exercise, the child must sit comfortably with their eyes closed, take a deep breath in through their nose, and hold that breath for seven seconds and release it slowly through their mouth. They should repeat this breathing exercise 10 times.

Walking briskly around the yard or playground can be used as a coping tool when the child has reached their frustration tolerance and needs to deal with intense emotions and release them in a healthy way. All they have to do is walk briskly around the house or the school in order to release pent-up aggression and energy. When they come back from the brisk walk, they will be calm and ready to face a new task. Such tasks don't have to be done one at a time; they can be done in combination, or however your child feels comfortable in performing them.

Strategies for Enforcing Rules and Clear Boundaries (Punishment and Rewards)

It is important to establish structure and boundaries for children who have ADHD, both in the home and at school. The child will thrive on discipline and structure, and they need clear and healthy boundaries to overcome their disorder. This means that parents need to set boundaries for their children and not renege on them when things get heated. It's easy to forget about discipline when it comes to a child who has special needs, but they need it just as much as a child who doesn't have special needs. If parents employ consistent strategies to create boundaries for their child, then they will get accustomed to these boundaries and respect them automatically over time.

It is difficult to stick to boundaries because they are hard to enforce. When a person sticks to the boundaries they have set, it usually causes tantrums and aggressive outbursts. The pushback doesn't mean the boundary is bad, and a parent should not feel bad if the reception is not a good one. Perseverance with the boundaries set will be the determining factor if those boundaries remain or not. Boundaries are essential for the emotional health and well-being of the entire family, and there are a few strategies to employ in order to enforce boundaries that are clear and effective on the child.

Be Specific

The rules in the house must be clear, and the child should know exactly what is expected of them. This can be done by making a chart of demerits and achievements where it can be tracked when the child has misbehaved or when the child has followed the rules and boundaries of the home. A chart like this can be beneficial, as it will track whether the child has been behaving well or badly over a certain period of time, and the parent may be able to dig further to see if they are experiencing a larger issue outside of the home.

Giving the child a list of rules will also hammer down the specifics of what is expected of them. Keep it simple but specific so that the child is aware of rules at the dinner table for example, or rules when they play outside or when they have company. It doesn't hurt to give the child gentle verbal reminders on what they are supposed to be doing. If the child is misbehaving, then it is encouraged for the parent to reprimand the child whilst explaining where they are going wrong. The parents should communicate as clearly as they can so that the child can understand the rules and boundaries being set.

The parents and caregivers of the child must be of one mind when it comes to what the rules and boundaries are. They must parent the same, and the rules should not change because one parent is not there. If mom is not home, the bedtime of the child should not change from what it usually is. The parent who does not follow the rules and boundaries set for the child is undoing all the work that is meant to benefit their child.

Don't Set Boundaries You Cannot Enforce

If a parent sets up a demerit system in which five demerits result in the child getting 15 minutes in the naughty corner, then the child should go to the naughty corner for 15 minutes when they receive the fifth demerit. It should not be up for negotiation, and parents should not hesitate or flinch to enforce the consequences. If a parent cannot respect their own rules and boundaries, they are teaching their children that they need not respect the rules and boundaries. The types of boundaries and rules set by the parents should be worth the hard work it requires to enforce them.

Praise the Child When Boundaries are Respected

Positive reinforcement can go a long way in changing a child's behavior. Parents need not only punish to teach a lesson, but also to reward when a lesson is learned. If parents have set the rules that toys must be picked up before bedtime and the child has done that without being reminded, that needs to be praised. Anything along the lines of "Wow! You must be so proud that you picked up your toys all on your own! Good job!" or "You have done a wonderful job picking up your toys, I couldn't have done it better!" will suffice.

It takes time for boundaries to be respected, but if you stick to the consequences set for violating them then over time, you'll start to see them being respected. Enforce consequences for the violations consistently so that when you praise the child for respecting the boundaries, it will motivate them to keep sticking to them. The more you reward the child for respecting boundaries, the more the child will maintain said respect.

Explain the Why

Forcing a child to respect rules and boundaries that are backed by the reason 'because I said so' will not motivate the child to learn to respect rules and boundaries. Playing old-school methods of parenting where the parents word supersedes that of the child because one is the parent and one is the child will not help the child's understand why the rules and boundaries are there in the first place. The child with ADHD needs to be sensitized on a lot of things, because most of them go over their heads as it is difficult to process a lot of information at once.

The parent should explain ADHD, what it is, and why they need the rules and boundaries in the home. The parents can give an example of school and how there are rules and boundaries at school that the child has to follow in order to learn effectively. Similarly, the parents could explain how the house has to run in a certain way, and as a member of the home, the child needs to abide by the rules set by the adults. The child needs to understand that the rules and boundaries are there for their benefit, even if it may not feel like they are.

CHAPTER 10

A PRACTICAL ACTION PLAN TO HELP

OUR CHILD

It can be daunting to accept an ADHD diagnosis. It may rouse feelings of inadequacy and self-blame. A parent may be relieved to finally know what is wrong with their child, but the diagnosis may also bring feelings of dread. No one is happy about changing their lives or incurring additional costs due to medical expenses. The dread can cause friction in the family, creating rifts because the parents are constantly frustrated with the circumstances they find themselves in.

If parents have a rough roadmap of how to navigate the first few weeks after the diagnosis, then it will be easy for them to get into a rhythm that would be beneficial for their child. The trick is to find that rhythm as soon as possible so that the child can begin to accrue the benefits of the treatment sooner. Up until the diagnosis, the child has been living in a state of anxiety and confusion, so the goal should be to try to give them peace and tools to deal with their symptoms.

Rachel did not know what she was going to do. The idea of adjusting her life very drastically was something she was hesitant to do. For years, Rachel had put blood, sweat, and tears into building her career. It was not fair that when Harvey's disorder came along, all of that went away. Either she poured all of herself into an action plan, or her life would get consumed by ADHD. To conquer this disorder, a plan needs to be formulated and followed meticulously.

Advantages of Having an Action Plan

There are multiple benefits of creating an action plan to deal with ADHD. One of the benefits is clarity; the disorder can come so quick and fast that it can be overwhelming for the affected child as well as their family. The clarity of the action plans means that the parents will not repeat previous mistakes and build on lessons learned. An action plan gives clarity in the sense that it makes priorities clear and allows parents to focus their time and energy into those priorities.

Another benefit of creating a clear action is that it provides focus on what should be done. When a plan requires a parent to focus on positive reinforcement, they will understand that they should not bring any kind of negativity into disciplining their child. When focus is put on certain tasks, an action plan can also give you a step-by-step guide so that you can understand what is required to achieve the goals that you have set. The parent will also notice the strengths and weaknesses that they have and where they fall short.

Once the action plan is formulated and is being followed consistently, it becomes very easy to measure progress. The activities that the child is struggling with will be glaringly obvious, and it will give the parent a chance to consult with the child's doctors or their support group on how best to overcome the challenges that they are experiencing. With an action plan, the parent can track their pace and obstacles in order to see where improvements need to be made.

The action plan also provides motivation, as the parent is able to track where they come from and the progress that has been made. The parent can praise the child on the progress that has been made, as they will be able to see the improvements over the period of time that the action plan has been in place. Implementation of the action plan will not be perfect, but parents can be proud of the discipline and determination they employ to carry it out every day. There is pride in showing up for your child consistently, and the action plan will give that satisfaction that the parent is doing the right thing for their child.

Things to Look Out For

Sometimes, the parents of the child can become obsessed with creating the perfect plan and become too engrossed in the details. The point is not to fuss over the details, but just to get started, hammering out other details along the way. The anxiety that comes with not knowing what you are doing can result in procrastination, which might prolong the planning process to avoid getting started. This is something to avoid. Draft what you can and start the action plan that will assist in the treatment of your child.

Once the action plan has been formulated, the parents may not want to keep educating themselves. They may descend into a state of complacency; they may feel like because they did the bare minimum, they need not do anything more. The child is constantly evolving and developing, however, so the parents need to always review if the action plan is still suitable for the child. For example, if the child's ADHD presentation has changed and they are now exhibiting a combined presentation, the parent has to pivot and re-adjust the daily activities to help improve the child's new symptoms. Research in the medical field is always being published, meaning what is fact today may change tomorrow. Due to this uncertainty, parents must not become complacent, but continue to improve upon the knowledge they have gained about ADHD.

The action plan needs to be followed consistently by the parents and the child, and it requires discipline in order to see some of the symptoms alleviated. This may lead to a parent being inflexible in responding to changes. Being stubborn to change is not always a good thing, as inflexibility often leads to frustration and control issues. Parents can quickly get into a negative headspace if the plan they formulated is not being followed or there are hiccups along the way. Inflexibility leads to the parent feeling stressed and as if they are failing, but the fact that there is an action plan and that the parent is trying to implement it is enough to show that the parent is trying. Compassion and flexibility are important factors in accepting that life does not always go to plan.

Creativity in solving problems will make dealing with ADHD a lot easier. Children who have ADHD are more intuitive and creative, and they may appreciate this type of problem-solving from their parents. Unfortunately, having a set routine, consistent structure, and an action plan may kill creativity. Everything that needs to be done is listed out and there is no wiggle room for spontaneity. To avoid having a boring action plan, leave some room to get creative or change the plan regularly to allow for diversity of activities. Get creative in the types of meals prepared; if the meal is chicken with vegetables, find different ways to prepare the meal.

Tips for Creating an Effective Action Plan

Create realistic and simple goals for the child to achieve. Do not be overly ambitious with these goals, as failing may discourage the child. A simple goal, like wanting your child to be able to sit still for long enough to finish their snack, is a good place to start then you build up from there. Create small and achievable milestones that will easily add up to larger accomplishments.

Create a vision and break it down to manageable steps in order to make it easy to take one step at a time to get there.

Time each activity so that the child is motivated to beat the clock. All goals need to be time-bound so that they are completed within a reasonable amount of time. 20 minutes for meal times is a reasonable amount of time, and five minutes for a shower can be the yardstick with which to measure timeframes needed. Every child is different, so the times will differ according to each child.

When the parents are setting goals on the action plan, they should always put the child at the forefront of every decision they make. The parent should barely consider themselves when formulating the action plan, as it is not meant for them. They are the medium through which it is implemented, but it is largely for the progress of the child. Selflessness is key, and the parent should know that they will forgo their comforts in order to make sure the child is comfortable.

This to-do list is a summarization of the key points to follow in order to begin a new life that accommodates a child with ADHD. Some of the points are easy to implement, and some take a little more work, self-discipline, and consistency. The following are a few of the things that should be implemented right away should a child be diagnosed with ADHD:

- Take note of symptoms and concerns.

- Consult with the child's educators to note behavior at school.

- Appoint with a child psychiatrist or therapist who specializes in ADHD to assess the child accordingly.

- Create a treatment management plan.

- Learn about which symptoms of ADHD your child is

presenting with.

- Research on classroom interventions that provide your child access to specific rights at school, due to their ADHD.

- Inform teachers at school and get the child assessed for learning disabilities.

- Inform relevant family members and loved ones with the consent of the child.

- Explain to the child what the diagnosis means.

- Research and learn about any prescriptions given and their potential side effects.

- Research alternative treatments and options.

- Join a parental support group in the community or online.

- Find out if you or any family members have ADHD.

- Enroll in therapy sessions.

- Create a detailed plan of action for rules and boundaries in the home.

- Decide which tools your child could benefit from (anger management, impulse control, etc.) and plan daily activities around them.

- Keep a journal of the child's progress and share it with them.

CHAPTER 11

ADHD HOMEWORK

Children are peculiar creatures that soak up information like a sponge. However, this doesn't mean that the information must be shoved down their throats. It is easier for them to learn when they are relaxed and having fun. When we craft lessons around a game, children are more eager to take part. These games can be played at home or at school to aid in the child's mental development. Children with ADHD should not be thought of as mentally challenged, as they simply need to be taught differently. If they are given the attention and extra care they need, they will thrive just as well as a child without a disorder. Here, we will be focusing on games that stimulate and improve the functioning of the child's executive functions.

Neuro- and Psychomotor Activities for Preschool-age Children

Games

- A four-piece puzzle to improve planning: taking part in the puzzle, even if it has a few pieces, will require the child to think logically and plan where to put which piece of the puzzle. They will realize they can't force the pieces together and that they are supposed to fit in a certain way.

- Snakes and ladders to increase attention span: playing a game of snakes and ladders means that the child has to see it through till the end. This will require the child to watch and pay attention to how the game is played and whose turn it is to play. They will be able to pay attention for a longer period, as they'll be excited to see if they win.

- Matching card game to improve memory: take five pairs of matching cards (10 cards total) and face them down to hide their numbers. Mix them up in front of the child and ask them to put the cards that match together. The child will have to remember where they saw a card that looked the same as the card they have in hand.

- Musical statue to improve impulsivity: this game involves running around and dancing when the music is playing, then standing still like a statue when the music is suddenly stopped. It is not easy to stop on command when the music stops playing. A game like this will improve self-control and impulsiveness, as it requires the child to become still regardless of what motion they were in.

Activities

- Being taught how to wash something to improve planning: when you teach a child how to wash their underwear or a small cloth, then they learn how to plan. A toddler is not able to do loads of laundry, but at Montessori schools, they teach young children how to wash a piece of clothing. They learn that you have to get a bowl with soapy water and a bowl with plain water, and from there, they learn that you start with the soapy water to remove the dirt and then rinse it out with the plain water. This activity teaches the child to plan out what they will be doing, and the order they will be doing it in.

- Being read a bedtime story to improve attention span: with a screen, the child can use their eyes to follow what is happening. A bedtime story requires that the child apply their focus to what is being said and following along. If the child zones out, they may lose what the plot is about; if the story is engaging, the child will pay extra attention to what is being said so they don't miss out on anything. This activity allows the child the opportunity to stretch out their attention span and themselves focused for longer, which improves their attention span.

- Recalling rules to improve memory: when a child is moving onto a new task or chore, the parent can ask the child to recall what the rules are. For example, if they are sitting at the dinner table, the parent could ask the child what the rules at the table are. If the child is able to recall them perfectly, they should be praised. If they are not able to remember all the rules, they should be reminded what they are and given a chance to re-iterate them back. This exercise allows the child to recall things they were told previously, helping to exercise their memory.

- Count to three before answering to improve impulsiveness: A parent should teach a child to always count to three before they want to speak. The child will usually not know how to stop themselves from interrupting others, but with this activity, they will be forced to stop themselves from responding and count to three. Only after they have counted to three may they respond. This is a great tool for children to assess if their response comes at an appropriate time or not.

Neuro- and Psychomotor Activities for Children 6-to-12

Games

- Maze games to improve planning: when a child is playing a game where they have to plan out their route not to reach a dead end in the maze, they are developing their planning skills. The child has to analyze the maze and see which route will lead them to the other side of the maze. Sometimes they pick the wrong route and they reach a dead end, which will also teach the child that they can regroup and try again. This type of game assists in learning how to plan, because the child will have to consider various options before they make a decision.

- Paddleball for improving attention span: paddleball is not an easy game to play, which is why it is for older kids and adults. A ball is attached to a paddle with a string, and with sufficient wrist action, a person hits the ball against the pedal over and over again. This game requires a lot of attention, as a certain rhythm must be maintained.

- Sequence games to improve memory: during these types of games, the child needs to recall a certain pattern of shapes and repeat the same patterns. This makes the child remember long sequences of patterns. During this game, the child is improving their memory and making their brain remember more and more sequences.

- Yoga to improve impulsivity: this type of exercise allows children to perform certain poses that require concentration and self-control. The child will have to be deliberate about the movement of their body in order to complete the yoga poses. This encourages the child to think before they act and not move impulsively as they are accustomed to do. Yoga can also be challenging, so it will provide the child with stimulation of the mind as well.

Activities

- Preparing meals to teach planning: as a child grows older, they need to learn life skills, one of which being cooking. Teaching children to prepare meals that are age-appropriate is important to teach them how to plan. For example, an eight year old can be reasonable for preparing their own cereal. They need to know that before they pour their cereal, they need to get a bowl and spoon, as well as the cereal and the milk. Planning ahead to have all the ingredients, cutlery, and crockery ready is essential as the child performs this task. Preparing meals such as sandwiches, desserts, and beverages could also teach the child to improve their planning skills.

- Reading to improve attention span: reading improves cognitive skills, because while you are reading, your neurons are making new connections in your brain. As you are reading, you are improving your attention span and learning new things. When you read a book, chapter one is related to chapter two, chapter two is related to chapter three and so forth; therefore, you have to pay attention to what is written throughout each chapter in order for the entire book to make sense. This activity is very beneficial in assisting the improvement of a child's attention span.

- Ask your child to teach you something they learned that day to improve memory: when your child gets home from school, ask them to teach you something that they may have learned that day. The child would have to recall a new concept or idea that they were taught that day and explain it in their own words. Recalling and repeating something from memory reinforces it in the child's mind and improves their recollection of that concept. This activity will also assist the child to recognize loopholes or errors in their recollection.

- Enroll the child in a sport to improve impulsivity: the more a child is trained to put thought behind every action they take, the less they will act without thinking. In every sport a person partakes in, they have to think about each and every move they make and the type of consequences that action will have. This will assist the child in understanding that they have to act only after thinking it through and what the possible ramifications will be.

Extensive focus must be placed on developing the child's executive functions so that their planning, attention, memory, and impulse control are all significantly improved by the games and activities they partake in. The games and activities listed above should be carried out consistently for a few weeks in order for a difference to be seen in the behavior of the child. There is no guarantee that these activities or games will be effective the first time around, so an open mind must be kept, as well as a curiosity to try different things.

Unnecessary pressure should not be placed on the child to perform these games and activities perfectly or in record time, as the end result is not what the activity is about. The neurological connections and development of the child's brain is what is key; it is about the process of these activities, rather than the end result. It is through this step-by-step that the child's executive functions will improve. Activities must always be lighthearted and fun so that the child can gain the benefits of the activities while also feeling relaxed and comfortable. Patience is a virtue that should never run out.

ADHD and Video Games

There are many myths and stigmas connected to ADHD, and a lot of them have been proven wrong. One of those myths is that video games actually cause ADHD. Parents can be confused as to why children fail to sit still long enough to eat a snack or to do their homework, or why they fail to listen to instruction, yet somehow they are able to sit for hours on end playing video games. There is no research studies that have concluded that there is a link between playing video games and developing ADHD. This does not explain why children are able to focus on them for so long and not in their daily lives.

The reason why children can focus on a video game and not in real life has to do with what is happening on the screen during the video game. Whether the child is playing Call of Duty or Mario Kart, something is always happening on the screen. Due to this constant movement and action, the child has to respond almost immediately or the lack of response will cause them to lose. The screen is action-packed and engaging, so they are in a constant state of stimulation.

Within the video game, there are mini-missions that the child has to complete, and they usually don't last for that long. The parents see the child sitting there for hours and think that they have been focused on one thing, when in reality they have been focused on a number of different tasks. Although video games are not a cause of ADHD, it is not recommended for a child to spend too much time playing them.

If your child can't stop playing video games, you can help them develop better focus working memory and improve upon their executive functions as a whole if you choose the right video game to play. We would like a child with ADHD to develop improved executive functions, and they can do so if the right game is chosen. While the child is playing, engage them and ask them what they think the problem is and how they think they can solve it. Once the child has identified what skills are necessary and how to overcome the problem, challenge them to identify where the skills are used in real life. Try to apply the newly-learned skills in a task around the house to demonstrate how the skills are used. Games like Minecraft, Roblox, and Bad Piggies are examples of good video games for teaching these methods.

CHAPTER 12

MEDICAL TREATMENT AND THERAPY

ADHD is a medical condition, meaning it needs medical intervention. The kind of medical intervention needed will vary from case to case, but the treatment that is followed the world over usually involves medication and therapy. Some parents don't like the idea of putting the child on medication once they are diagnosed with ADHD. What will work for the child will depend on the child's age and their socioeconomic status, their environmental factors, and the types of symptoms they are presenting. There is no blueprint on what exactly should be applied to each child, so the parents should work closely with the doctors to see what is the best course of action.

The AAP prefers to try behavior management as the first line of treatment when a child is below the age of six. When the child is over six years old, they can be prescribed medication as well as behavior management. If the child is going to school, then the school should also be involved in behavioral classroom intervention and providing support to the child in whatever way they need it during school time. It is important to note that it is not only the parents who are involved in the child's treatment, but their educators as well.

There are two types of medications usually prescribed for children who have ADHD, those being stimulants and non-stimulants. Stimulants are more popularly used, and they act quickly and reduce ADHD symptoms faster, whereas non-stimulants are newer in the market, work slower than stimulants, but can stay in the system for up to 24 hours. Medication will always have side effects, and ADHD medication is no different, with side effects including disturbances in sleep and suppressed appetite. Children may not respond well to medicine, and healthcare providers may need to try different medications at different doses to see what will work for that child.

The types of medicine that are used to treat ADHD today do not serve as a cure, but as treatment plans. The first type of medicine is methylphenidate. It is categorized as a stimulant, and it is the most prescribed medicine for ADHD. This medication increases brain activity in the areas that are responsible for controlling behavior and attention. It can be prescribed for children over the age of five, and it can be taken in small doses two-to-three times a day. Methylphenidate comes in two types of tablets; immediate release, which is taken more often in the day, or modified-release tablets that release small doses throughout the day. Side effects include trouble sleeping, loss of appetite, increased blood pressure and feelings of aggression, irritability, anxiety, and depression.

Another commonly used medication is lisdexamfetamine. Although it is only prescribed after a minimum of six weeks of methylphenidate use has not improved symptoms, it is a stimulant that improves focus and concentration while suppressing impulsive behavior. It is prescribed for children over the age of five, and it comes in capsule form to be ingested only once in the day. In adults, it is the medicine of choice over methylphenidate. Common side effects include suppressed appetite, drowsiness, aggression, vomiting, nausea, and diarrhea.

The next medicine that the child is prescribed is dexamfetamine; it is also prescribed to children over the age of five who have been diagnosed with ADHD. It is taken two to four times a day in tablet form, but it can also be prescribed as an oral solution if necessary. The side effects of dexamphetamine include mood swings, aggression, dizziness, headaches, vomiting and nausea, mood swings, and decreased appetite.

Atomoxetine is a selective noradrenaline reuptake inhibitor which increases a chemical in the brain called noradrenaline. By increasing this chemical in the brain, it increases levels of concentration as well as adding in controlling impulses. The reason why it increases concentration is that noradrenaline is responsible for passing messages between brain cells. This is the third option after methylphenidate and lisdexamfetamine being ineffective in the child, and is recommended for children over five years of age. This medication is taken once a day in capsules. Common side effects of atomoxetine include a slight increase in heart rate and blood pressure, vomiting, nausea, tummy aches, and insomnia. Unfortunately, there are more serious side effects that have been reported with the use of atomoxetine, such as the liver damage and suicidal thoughts. If depression is suspected in the child, it is important to mention it to their doctor.

Guanfacine is a medication that reduces blood pressure, but can also be used to improve attention, as it acts on the specific part of the brain that is responsible for focus. This medication is offered to children over five years old, but should not be prescribed for adults. If for some reason methylphenidate or lisdexamfetamine cannot be used, then guanfacine is the next option. It comes in tablet form and can be used either in the morning or in the evening. The side effects for this medication are tiredness, abdominal pain, dry mouth, and headache.

There are various ways to medically treat ADHD, and it's important for the child's caregivers to be aware of the options that are available to them. A majority of the time when a child is diagnosed with ADHD, the parent is ignorant of what the disorder is and what it means for the child and their family. Applying treatment as prescribed is a lifelong journey that both the parent and the child must be committed to. If treatment is followed as prescribed, the child can lead a normal and fulfilling life that is not hindered by their ADHD symptoms.

Psychotherapy

Psychotherapy is described as the treatment of mental health issues by engaging with, speaking to, and confiding in a psychiatrist, psychologist, or any other mental health therapist. This type of therapy has been said to be beneficial with or without medication. There are different types of psychotherapy that can be used to treat ADHD and they include, but are not limited to, behavioral therapy, cognitive behavioral therapy for adolescents, and ADHD coaching. Psychotherapy can be provided not only to the child, but also to their parents, their families, or even their teacher, in an effort to educate and empower the child's support system.

Play therapy can be used to assist a child who has ADHD by providing a comfortable place for them to freely express themselves. When a child is at play, they are able to learn and connect with who they are playing with. The therapist will be able to assess how the child thinks and behaves; during play sessions, the therapist will also be able to soothe the child's anxieties and frustrations. The aim of play therapy is to give the child reassurance that they will conquer their ADHD, as well as provide encouragement to increase their self-esteem.

Psychotherapy is not the only type of therapy used to treat ADHD in children. There is dialectical behavior therapy, brain training, music therapy, art therapy, and equine therapy; the sky's the limit on which type of therapy is appropriate for the child. It may take some time to figure out what works and what doesn't work, but there should be an effort to explore what produces the best results in the child. Therapy is always beneficial to the child, and will never be a disadvantage whether or not the child is on medication.

Non-pharmacological Therapy

Behavioral Therapy

Behavioral therapy acts as a preventative measure to deal with behavioral problems caused by ADHD symptoms. From the perspective of this type of therapy, it is better to enforce structure predictability and routine in order to reduce problems caused by the disorder. Behavioral therapy also employs the use of increased positive attention on the child in order to reinforce their self-esteem and provide reassurance to the child.

A good behavioral therapy plan that aims to treat ADHD should include the following aspects:

- A reward system to provide productive reinforcement for good behavior. This shows the child that if they keep behaving well, they will keep getting rewarded. In certain instances, it also shows the child that the longer they behave well, the bigger their reward.

- Minimize the occurrence of triggers. By minimizing the triggers of negative behavior, the parent gives the child a chance to develop in a safe and calm environment. Not paying attention to what triggers the child will leave them in a constant state of frustration, confusion, and anxiety. When they are in this state, it leaves room for negative behaviors to creep in and dominate their behavior.

- Negative behavior from the child being ignored by the adult. The reason this is important is that some of the behaviors that children with ADHD exhibit are purely for attention-seeking. Negative behaviors are ignored so that the child is discouraged from behaving that way.

- Remove privileges if negative behavior persists. This aspect of behavioral therapy is almost the reverse of the reward system. When the child is consistently exhibiting negative behavior, then they should have a privilege taken away to show them that negative behavior attracts unpleasant consequences.

Behavioral therapy is heralded as one of the most effective types of therapy to treat the poor symptoms of ADHD. Unfortunately, the success of behavioral therapy depends on the parents' ability to consistently stick to the plan. If the parent is not able to be consistent with the plan set out for the child, then they will not see the results. Luckily, parents are also given support groups and tools to support them while they implement behavioral therapy.

Educational Interventions Aimed at Parents

The success of treatments prescribed to children who have ADHD are hinged on the self-discipline and commitment of their parents. If we look at Rachel as an example of a committed parent, we are able to see that she gave her whole life in the pursuit of making Harvey better. Not every parent is able to make that much of a sacrifice, but they have to give the same kind of commitment in order to implement prescribed strategies. To see progress, ADHD treatment has to be consistent. When parents have limited access to information or don't attend therapy sessions, it becomes a hindrance in the progress of the child.

Parent training and educational programs are there to specifically sensitize parents and educate them in how they are supposed to communicate with their child, as well as how to collaborate with the child in order to effectively improve their behavior. This type of training can be given to a parent well before the child is officially diagnosed with ADHD. This is done so that when the parent is given the diagnosis, they are well prepared to carry out an action plan to treat the child. These programs are there to support parents of children who have ADHD, and they are not meant to bring shame to the parents or make them feel as if they are inadequate. These kinds of programs are taught by instructing a class consisting of roughly a dozen people in a group, with up to 16 meetings that are around two hours each. The end goal is to increase the confidence that a parent has in their ability to relate to their child, as well as providing skills to manage the child's ADHD.

Sometimes, parents don't have access to transport or financial resources that would allow them to attend physical therapy sessions with their child. In this case, education and resources should be available to the parent via the Internet on an online platform. This way, if a parent cannot attend physically, then they still have the option to access that kind of information online. The parents need to be provided with literature on various effective methods of behavioral therapy, and they should also be provided with feedback from the parents that have tried that specific course of action.

Once the program implementation is in place, parents should have a way to give feedback and revise implementation of the program. The revised program will then be implemented, and parents will have a chance to give feedback once again. The blueprint is not always perfect and will not always work for every child, which is why there is such a need for revisions and feedback. This also educates and desensitizes the parent to the fact that ADHD is a lifelong struggle, and what works today might not work tomorrow.

The National Resource Center (NRC) on ADHD funds a program called Children and Adults with Attention-Deficit/Hyperactivity Disorder (CHADD) that supports children who have ADHD, as well as their parents. There is an ocean of information about

ADHD and how to manage it, but what is noteworthy about CHADD is that they also provide tips and education for parents of children who have the disorder. There is also a section about understanding ADHD more specifically for parents and caregivers. Utilizing a resource like this will help to give educational interventions that will support the parents of a child with ADHD.

Cognitive Behavioral Therapy

A short-term type of psychotherapy is cognitive behavioral therapy, which attempts to eliminate negative thoughts and beliefs by changing thought patterns. This type of therapy is geared toward adults and adolescents because they can be made aware of their negative thinking patterns. Unfortunately, this type of therapy does not treat the symptoms that will accompany ADHD presentations of hyperactivity, impulsiveness, and inattention. Cognitive behavioral therapy eliminates generalizations, comparisons, and the psychological impulse to magnify your shortcomings while minimizing your accomplishments.

Healthy and Balanced Diet

Good nutrition is at the center of good living. Without good nutrition, a person opens themselves up to unnecessary ailments and diseases. In addition to medication and therapy, it is important for any child with ADHD to maintain good nutrition. The responsibility for good nutrition falls on the parents, and they need to understand that a healthy balanced diet is important in alleviating symptoms of ADHD. A good nutrition is a complementary feature in trying to suppress service symptoms of ADHD and provide a balanced life for the child.

There are certain foods that are thought to aggravate ADHD symptoms, such as sugar and AFCs. Home-cooked meals are preferred over fatty salty takeout that will only worsen the health of the child. A diet rich in healthy fats, fruits, vegetables, and appropriate starches will ensure that the child is receiving the necessary nutrients. Observing a child after they eat certain things could also provide clues as to which specific foods create triggers for their ADHD.

There are numerous resources online that can provide recipes that are quick and simple to prepare for children who have ADHD. For example, CHADD has a cookbook for busy minds which is a simple, easy, and healthy meal plan to feed the brain. Protein-rich breakfasts are said to be beneficial for people who have ADHD, as it boosts performance and the attention span of the child while simultaneously reducing depression and anxiety. A breakfast that is rich in carbohydrates does little to improve a child's hyperactivity. For breakfast, consider peanut butter on whole grain bread, plain yogurt with fresh fruit, or hard-boiled eggs, toast and fruit; the options are limitless.

The snacks that should be given to children who have ADHD should not include energy drinks, soda, or fruity juices that have AFCs or sweeteners. The parents should aim for high-fiber snacks that have low sugar content, such as popcorn, veggie sticks with tasty dips, dried fruits and nuts, fresh fruit, and crackers with cheese. These kinds of snacks maintain the child's energy levels and stabilize blood sugar as the day goes by. A child can have two snacks a day, with the first one being between breakfast and lunch and the second one between lunch and dinner. Snacks are not meant to be felt, meaning their quantity should not be the same size as a meal.

At dinner time, the parents should focus on giving the child as much omega-3 fatty acids as possible. Omega-3 fatty acids are said to improve ADHD symptoms, so they should be given in abundance. To increase their presence, parents should give children more tuna, salmon walnuts, chia seeds, olive oil, and canola oil. Dinner can include cauliflower mac & cheese, chicken enchiladas, sesame salmon burgers, and rosemary lemon chicken. The idea is to give the child options and varieties so that they are not bored with the types of meals they are given on a daily basis.

Quick and simple desserts for ADHD children that may have food sensitivities include fresh fruit salad, baked banana with honey, raspberry purée over yogurt, or baked apples with cinnamon. These desserts cater to children who may have adverse reactions to additives, AFCs, preservatives, and artificial flavorings. If the dessert can be fresh, it is better for the child; try to also avoid simple carbohydrates such as products made with white flour or white rice and substitute them with complex carbohydrates, like whole wheat flour, brown rice, and oatmeal. The specifics of the meal will depend on the financial capability of the parents; cheaper alternatives to expensive products are always available.

Supplements

A supplement is a basic nutrient that aids health and bodily function that a person may not be receiving from their daily meals. Supplements could be anything from minerals, vitamins, fats, or proteins. Think of a bodybuilder who takes protein supplements in order to grow their muscle mass, as they can't eat the large amount of protein needed that will result in the large swollen muscles that they require. There are numerous supplements in the world, but only a few are said to improve the symptoms of ADHD. Supplements are an option that a parent could use to complement the child's prescribed treatment for

ADHD, but in no way are supplements a treatment by themselves. When parents are seeking to introduce supplements into a child's diet, it is important to notify the child's doctor.

There are certain supplements that are theorized to give the body a boost and aid in easing the symptoms of ADHD. One such supplement is polyunsaturated fatty acid, which can be found in products like fish oil. Research has been done on whether there is a link between taking polyunsaturated fatty acid and improvement of ADHD symptoms, and the results are mixed. Even though more research needs to be conducted to reach a definitive conclusion, it doesn't hurt to give children polyunsaturated fatty acid as a supplement. Fatty acid supplementation is no match for therapy and medication when it comes to FDA-approved treatment for ADHD.

Iron is crucial for brain development and function, yet it is one of the minerals that can be in shortage in a child with ADHD. Blood tests should be done to measure the child's iron that goes before taking iron supplements. Multivitamins go a long way in assisting in a wide range of vitamins and minerals. When a child is given a balanced and healthy diet, then this becomes a complementary precaution to ensure they do not develop any kind of deficiency. There are multivitamins designed for children with ADHD, but they tend to be more expensive than the regular kind.

There are certain herbs that are considered beneficial to children who have ADHD, including chamomile, spearmint, and lemongrass. These types of herbal supplements can be used during bedtime by either rubbing them on the wrists and temples of the child in the form of essential oils or given to the child as a warm beverage. Another herbal remedy that is said to stimulate brain function, as well as boost energy, is ginseng. It is said to ease anxiety and social functioning of a child who has issues in those areas. Pine bark extract is said to stabilize antioxidant levels in children as well as reduce hyperactivity; this herbal supplement also aids in improving attention span and concentration because it includes pycnogenol, which lowers stress hormones.

Ginkgo biloba is a popular herb that has been hailed for its ability to improve cognitive function. Due to the fact that children with ADHD struggle with executive functions, this herb can be beneficial in pacifying the effects of the disorder and increasing attention span. As with all supplements, the body can only absorb so much, and the benefits will only be evident after three months. If the child is on medication, then it is best to consult their doctor when introducing multivitamins to make sure that the multivitamins do not counteract or cause a bad reaction.

Keep an Open Mind

It seems almost unnatural to have your child on medication before they have reached adolescence, but it is important for parents to keep an open mind if they want their child to get better. Adopting a supportive stance toward medication prescribed to your child will also allow them to be more accepting of the changes. If a parent is displaying hostile or negative energy when it comes to the issue of medication, the child would be reluctant to take it. Parents must explain why it is important for the child to consistently take their medication, and they should also explain what the medication is for and the effect it will have on the child.

The parent should keep an eye on the child for adverse side effects of the medication, and they should also speak to the child about how the medication is treating them. With time, the child will be able to articulate if the medication doesn't make them feel good. If one medication has adverse side effects, then the doctor will change the medication. Medications may also change depending on the type of ADHD presentation and the symptoms that child is showing. There is no shame in taking medication for ADHD as long as the child is getting better.

CONCLUSION

There is light at the end of the tunnel, and the child can be at peace if parents persevere and give them a chance at a normal life. Rachel was not sure if she could take on the large responsibility of parenting a child who has ADHD. She was afraid and insecure; she never thought that she and Mike would be parents to a child who had special needs. Rachel soon realized that although Harvey had ADHD, he was still her sweet little boy that she had loved from the day he was born. Nothing the disorder did could ever make Rachel stop at loving Harvey the way that she had loved him since birth.

Rachel had to identify which actions were Harvey acting out and which actions were the ADHD. When a child is young, it is quite difficult to differentiate between symptoms of ADHD and normal childish behavior. Rachel had to suppress her frustrations, anger, and impatience in order to see that Harvey needed help. Relying on her instinct as a mother and what she saw Harvey go through every day, she knew that she had to provide him an opportunity to get better. As is often seen demonstrated every day, a mother's love knows no bounds, and Rachel went to the ends of the earth for Harvey to the point where she changed careers in order to understand her son better.

With the knowledge that she has accrued, she wants to make the lives of children with ADHD better by teaching their parents how to deal with the disorder in a healthy and constructive manner. That is why you are reading this book today, and why you will begin to apply the methods and advice written throughout the chapters in this guide. Gone are the days where children are expected to keep quiet and do as they're told without reason. Positive parenting involves communicating with the child and giving them reasons why we do things. A child with ADHD needs to understand why things are the way they are, and why they are structured and rules are put in place for their development.

Rachel could've easily given up and decided not to take an active role in the treatments prescribed for her child. Mike could've been the one to take Harvey to his therapy sessions or to be the one to enact the behavioral therapy plan. Fortunately for Harvey, this was not the case. The fact that Rachel took an active decision to go the extra mile for her son is why he had a fighting chance to lead a normal life. With this guide, you too can give your child a chance at leading a normal life.

Chapter by chapter, we defined what ADHD is, went through the presentations and the symptoms, and explained when ADHD begins. Just like how Rachel went through a phase of educating herself and becoming an expert on what ADHD is and what it means for the child who is affected by it, this guide has also given you the knowledge you need to be an expert. We hope after receiving this information, you will be inspired to arm yourself with even more education on what the disorder means for your family and your child.

By going through major difficulties that a child may face at school and at home, we hope it has sensitized you to what the child is constantly struggling with. To imagine what a child with ADHD experiences every day is near impossible, but we have to attempt to put ourselves in their shoes in order to have compassion and sympathy for them and the torment they experience. Rachel's heart was broken watching what Harvey was going through day in and day out. The torture is real, but it is only experienced by the child.

Unlike other diseases and ailments, you can't see with your eyes where exactly your child is hurting or needs healing. Sometimes, the child is unable to even express what is wrong. All the parent can see is tears, outbursts, and negative behavior. Only after noticing glaring problems in the behavior of the child over a period of time, in various settings, can the parent then definitively say that there is something wrong with the child. How long was the child experiencing symptoms of confusion and frustration before it was noticed by adults around them?

Life doesn't occur in a vacuum. There are various other circumstances that could present themselves along with ADHD, and both the child and the parents need to roll with the punches. It is possible that the child could have developed a co-occurring disorder, experienced trauma, or have learning disabilities. The parents would need to trade the co-occurring disorder as well as the ADHD; they cannot treat one and leave the other behind. A person needs to be flexible enough to take what life is throwing at them.

There is no giving up allowed. Giving up means that the disorder wins. Giving up means that your child is not going to get relief from the constant torture of living with ADHD. Imagine Rachel who had a career that she loved and excelled in and had to give it up to take care of her son. She made a sacrifice that was fitting to her situation and her life, just like you will make a sacrifice for your child that is fitting to your life in order for them to get better. Love is sacrifice. Let go of your past life and begin anew.

Your child is special, your child is capable, and your child is creative and intuitive. They can achieve anything they set their minds on achieving, they simply need the right tools to figure out how their minds work and how to make that work for them in daily life. It can be scary to hear the diagnosis at first, but you can do it, and you will get through it. This is the survival guide for children with ADHD. Go through the new approach we have set out that uses positive parenting to empower the child. With the skills set out in this book, you will give your child the tools needed to self-regulate and manage their symptoms and emotions.

Rachel is proud of you. Rachel is proud of the progress that you're making in the progress that your child is making. You and your child will overcome ADHD!

"I have gone through every difficult burden and survived. Sometimes I did not know if I was going to make it, but Mike, Harvey, and I all made it work. Today, Harvey is a bright confident young man who grabs life by the horns and goes for every opportunity that comes his way. He no longer feels overwhelmed by his social situation, and his outbursts occur less and less. With the tools that I have provided my son, he is now able to handle his frustrations and blow off steam in a healthy manner.

Academically, Harvey does his best because his educators are aware of his disorder and they support him at every turn. Harvey is aware that his mind functions differently from the minds of other children, but he knows this doesn't mean that he is any less intelligent than they are. Slowly, Mike and I started noticing an improvement in Harvey's academic performance, and now he is excelling in every subject. This progress has given him a renewed confidence in himself, and he now also wants to become a psychiatrist to help children who have ADHD. My proudest moment was when Harvey said he wanted to be just like me when he grows up.

I used to feel as if I was the problem and that I was not getting it right, but all it needed was some time. I needed time to figure out what worked and what didn't work. Harvey needed time to adjust to new schedules and diets and to see if they had any effect on his symptoms. I was so used to seeing results quickly that I forgot that I had to slow down and watch each and every action and the reaction that came from it. Things slowed down, and I had to take everything a day at a time. Some days were longer than others, and sometimes I just wanted to cry. Some days came with failure, and others came with success. There were times where I felt so alone that not even Mike could save me from myself.

In the end, every decision and every sacrifice I made was worth it. There is nothing that I want to do for my son and my husband. I hope you felt the love I have for them in every page of this book. I hope that you two will take all this information and use it to further express your love for your family. We can do nothing if we are not educated about what ADHD is and how it affects our children. I hope that after reading this book, you have gained new knowledge that will improve how you carry out your child's treatment.

In the beginning, people thought I was crazy. They thought I may have lost my mind to want to quit my job to dedicate myself to understanding ADHD and making Harvey better. They thought I was crazy to depend on Mike as the sole breadwinner so that I could take care of Harvey. Everything I did seemed unconventional, but I knew what I needed to do to help my son overcome his disorder. In the same way, I know that you have done what others considered crazy to keep your family happy, healthy, and together. Even if things are not working out, as long as you are doing your best, your children will appreciate you for it.

The world is filled with so much darkness, and I would like to provide a light through this book so that you can parent your child. It is time for your child to put the days filled with frustration and confusion behind them. It is time to increase their attention span and focus so that they do not get left behind developmentally. The time is now to help your child self-regulate. The time is now to be used as a tool for your child to survive ADHD!"

-Heartfelt hugs from Rachel

Thank you for reading this book.

If you enjoyed it, please visit the site where you purchased it and write a brief review. Your feedback is important to me and will help other readers decide whether to read the book too.

I LOVE YOU!

RACHEL ROSS

GLOSSARY

ADD: Attention Deficit Disorder

ADHD: Attention Deficit Hyperactivity Disorder

Anxiety disorder: any disorder based in fear, apprehension, and constant worry

Autism Spectrum Disorder: any of the neurodevelopmental disorders where communication, both verbal and non-verbal, is impaired as well social interactions; other characteristics include repetitive behaviors and narrowed interests

Behavioral therapy: a type of therapy that helps participants unlearn negative behaviors and instills positive ones

Capricious child: one who succumbs to sudden and unaccountable changes of mood or behavior

Cognitive flexibility: being able to assess and adapt actions to various situations

Conversion disorder: formerly known as hysteria; a disorder characterized by symptoms caused by psychological reasons

Conduct disorder: a disorder characterized by one having aggression towards others

Deficient emotional self-regulation: the inability for a person to regulate reactions to their emotions

DSM: Diagnostic and Statistical Manual of Mental Disorders

Dissociative disorders: any disorder that disrupts the normal processing of the environment via consciousness, memory, and perception

Emotional impulsiveness: risky actions that are taken without thought to consequences

Frontal lobe: the part of the brain responsible for executive and motor functions

Gene-environment interactions: when factors in the environment and genes interact in way that sparks disease or disorders

General practitioner: also called family practice doctors; are trained to treat various ailments in all members of the family

Hyperactive: being so full of energy that it is like the person is being run like a motor; this state usually interferes with the development of the person

Hyperkinetic disorder: the old name for ADHD

Impulsive: risky behavior that lacks forethought

Inattention: a condition where there is a deficit in focused attention or the inability to concentrate

Intellectual disability: limitations in cognitive function and adaptive behaviors; this term is more politically correct than saying mental retardation

Learning disorder: any disorder that prohibits sufficient neurological information synthesis expected for that age or education as per standardized tests

Mental disorder: when a sufferer experiences disturbance in their functioning, emotions, and/or behavior

Mood disorder: elongated emotional disturbances

Neurodevelopmental disorders: any disorder that begins in infancy that impair the mind and body's functioning

Neurodevelopmental motor disorders: any disorder that disturbs development in learning, controlling, and execution of a person's motor skills

Neurotransmitter: chemicals released by neurons to transmit signals between them

Neurologist: a doctor trained in treating disorders that the nervous system and the brain

Oppositional defiant disorder (ODD): a disorder characterized by constant angry outbursts or acting out

Pediatrician: a doctor trained in pediatrics, which is the branch of medicine that deals with the care of children

Personality disorder: disturbances in how a person perceives themselves and their surroundings that has long lasting negative effects on their lives and happen frequently

Psychiatrist: a doctor trained in mental, personality, and behavioral disorders; they diagnose and treat such disorders

Psychotic disorder: a mental affliction wherein the sufferer has an intense distortion of reality even with contrary evidence

Psychologist: a doctor trained in the field of psychology

Psychotherapy: therapy that requires talking and communication between a patient and their therapist

Rheumatoid arthritis: a disease that mainly attacks the joints; the immune system attacks healthy cells and causes inflammation

Schizophrenia: a psychotic disorder where cognitive functioning is disturbed; the behavior of the sufferer and their emotional responsiveness is also affected

Stimulants: what increases the excitement in an organism, resulting in increased functional activity

Tic disorders: any disorder where vocal or motor tics occur multiple times a day

Tourette's syndrome: a tic disorder with numerous motor and vocal tics

Trauma: a bad experience that causes last feelings of fear, confusion, and helplessness and affects a person's normal function and reasoning

REFERENCES

About RMTi - Rhythmic Movement. (n.d.). Rhythmic Movement Training International. Retrieved January 24, 2022, from https://www.rhythmicmovement.org/rmt-explained

ADDitude Editors. (2009, June 16). *Tuning Out Distractions, Focusing in on School. ADDitude*; ADDitude. https://www.additudemag.com/end-distractibility-improving-adhd-focus-at-home-and-school/

Adesman, A. R. (2001). The Diagnosis and Management of Attention-Deficit/Hyperactivity Disorder in Pediatric Patients. *Primary Care Companion to the Journal of Clinical Psychiatry, 3*(2), 66–77. https://www.ncbi.nlm.nih.gov/pmc/articles/PMC181164/

ADHD & the Brain. (2019). Aacap.org. https://www.aacap.org/AACAP/Families_and_Youth/Facts_for_Families/FFF-Guide/ADIID_and_the_Brain.aspx

ADHD Institute. (2016). *ADHD Epidemiology | ADHD Institute.* ADHD Institute. https://adhd-institute.com/burden-of-adhd/epidemiology/

ADHD Testing – Attention, Executive Functioning and Memory. (n.d.). Retrieved January 3, 2022, from https://www.mentalhelp.net/adhd/testing/executive-functioning-and-memory/

American Psychological Association. (n.d.-a). *APA Dictionary of Psychology.* Dictionary.apa.org. Retrieved December 30, 2021, from https://dictionary.apa.org/inattention

American Psychological Association. (n.d.-b). *Metacognition.* APA Dictionary of Psychology. https://dictionary.apa.org/metacognition

Anita, T. (2009). An Overview on the Genetics of ADHD. *Acta Psychologica Sinica, 40*(10), 1088–1098. https://doi.org/10.3724/sp.j.1041.2008.01088

APA Dictionary of Psychology. (n.d.-a). Dictionary.apa.org. Retrieved January 1, 2022, from https://dictionary.apa.org/psychiatrist

APA Dictionary of Psychology. (n.d.-b). Dictionary.apa.org. Retrieved January 1, 2022, from https://dictionary.apa.org/neurology

APA Dictionary of Psychology. (n.d.-c). Dictionary.apa.org. Retrieved January 1, 2022, from https://dictionary.apa.org/psychologist

APA Dictionary of Psychology. (n.d.-d). Dictionary.apa.org. https://dictionary.apa.org/therapist

APA Dictionary of Psychology. (n.d.-a). *Speech therapy.* APA Dictionary of Psychology. Retrieved January 10, 2022, from https://dictionary.apa.org/speech-therapy

APA Dictionary of Psychology. (n.d.-b). *Trauma.* APA Dictionary of Psychology. https://dictionary.apa.org/trauma

Banerjee, T. D., Middleton, F., & Faraone, S. V. (2007). Environmental risk factors for attention-deficit hyperactivity disorder. *Acta Paediatrica, 96*(9), 1269–1274. https://doi.org/10.1111/j.1651-2227.2007.00430.x

Barkley, R. A. (2020, October 11). *What is the relationship between ADHD and emotional regulation?* ADHD Awareness Month - October 2021. https://www.adhdawarenessmonth.org/adhd-and-emotional-regulation/

Brown, N. M. (2020, November 4). Childhood Trauma and ADHD: A Complete Overview & Clinical Guidance. *ADDitude.* https://www.additudemag.com/adhd-and-trauma-overview-signs-symptoms/

Brown, T. E. (n.d.). *ADHD and emotions.* Understood. https://www.understood.org/articles/en/adhd-and-emotions-what-you-need-to-know

Centers for Disease Control and Prevention. (2018). *Symptoms and diagnosis of ADHD.* Centers for Disease Control and Prevention. https://www.cdc.gov/ncbddd/adhd/diagnosis.html

CHADD. (2018a). *Parenting a Child with ADHD* - CHADD. CHADD. https://chadd.org/for-parents/overview/

CHADD. (2018b). *Preschoolers and ADHD.* CHADD. https://chadd.org/for-parents/preschoolers-and-adhd/

Conrad, P., & Potter, D. (2000). From Hyperactive Children to ADHD Adults: Observations on the Expansion of Medical Categories. *Social Problems*, 47(4), 559–582. https://doi.org/10.2307/3097135

DSM-5 ADHD SYMPTOM CHECKLIST. (n.d.). https://chsciowa.org/sites/chsciowa.org/files/resource/files/1_-_adhd_dsm-5_checklist.pdf

Edwards, J. (n.d.). *Routine screening needed to identify language problems in kids with ADHD*. ACAMH. Retrieved January 8, 2022, from https://www.acamh.org/research-digest/routine-screening-needed-identify-language-problems-children-adhd/

Faraone, S. V., Banaschewski, T., Coghill, D., Zheng, Y., Biederman, J., Bellgrove, M. A., & Wang, Y. (2021). The World Federation of ADHD International Consensus Statement: 208 Evidence-based Conclusions about the Disorder. *Neuroscience & Biobehavioral Reviews*. https://doi.org/10.1016/j.neubiorev.2021.01.022

Hartman, C. A., Rommelse, N., van der Klugt, C. L., Wanders, R. B. K., & Timmerman, M. E. (2019). Stress Exposure and the Course of ADHD from Childhood to Young Adulthood: Comorbid Severe Emotion Dysregulation or Mood and Anxiety Problems. *Journal of Clinical Medicine*, 8(11), 1824. https://doi.org/10.3390/jcm8111824

Howes, D. H. (n.d.). *What is collaborative problem solving for ADHD? | ADD/ADHD Treatment*. Sharecare. Retrieved January 20, 2022, from https://www.sharecare.com/health/add-adhd-treatment/what-collaborative-problem-solving-adhd

Hyperactive Children. (1973). *The British Medical Journal*, 1(5849), 305–306. https://www.jstor.org/stable/25424475

Kessler, Z. (2015, July 13). *ADHD and Adoption: The Connections Between Them*. ImpactParents. https://impactparents.com/blog/complex-kids/adhd-and-adoption-the-connections-between-them/

Kulman, R. (2014, November 3). *Video Games Can Help Kids with ADHD – If You Choose Wisely*. ADDitude. https://www.additudemag.com/video-games-help-adhd/

Lange, K. W., Reichl, S., Lange, K. M., Tucha, L., & Tucha, O. (2010). The history of attention deficit hyperactivity disorder. *ADHD Attention*

Deficit and Hyperactivity Disorders, 2(4), 241–255. https://doi.org/10.1007/s12402-010-0045-8

Laufer, M. W., & Denhoff, E. (1957). Hyperkinetic behavior syndrome in children. *The Journal of Pediatrics*, 50(4), 463–474. https://doi.org/10.1016/s0022-3476(57)80257-1

Leary, P. M. (2003). Conversion disorder in childhood—diagnosed too late, investigated too much? *Journal of the Royal Society of Medicine*, 96(9), 436–438. https://www.ncbi.nlm.nih.gov/pmc/articles/PMC539597/

Lillis, C. (2019, July 26). *ADHD triggers: What to know*. Medical News Today. https://www.medicalnewstoday.com/articles/325867#adhd-triggers

Low, K. (2008, April 12). *How Does Your ADHD Child Learn?* Verywell Mind. https://www.verywellmind.com/learning-styles-and-adhd-20551

Low, K. (2019, October 28). *Tips for Helping Your Child With ADHD to Stop, Listen, and Respond.* Verywell Mind. https://www.verywellmind.com/parenting-adhd-children-parenting-strategies-20543

Low, K. (2021a, April 12). *Your Guide to Understanding Anger in ADHD Children.* Verywell Mind. https://www.verywellmind.com/understanding-adhd-children-and-anger-20540

Low, K. (2021b, July 8). *How Parents Can Make an Easier Life for Their Child With ADHD.* Verywell Mind. https://www.verywellmind.com/understanding-children-with-adhd-20686

Mac, D. (2015, January 16). *The connection between ADHD, speech delays, motor skill delays, sensory processing disorders and sleep issues.* Counseling Today. https://ct.counseling.org/2015/01/the-connection-between-adhd-speech-delays-motor-skill-delays-sensory-processing-disorders-and-sleep-issues/

Margolis, C. (2017, September 4). *"FYI: You Are the Perfect Parent for Your Child."* ADDitude. https://www.additudemag.com/accepting-child-adhd-positive-parenting/

Mcilroy, A. T. (2018, August 10). *How to Increase Your Preschooler's Attention Span.* Empowered Parents. https://empoweredparents.co/10-ways-to-develop-your-preschoolers-concentration-span/

Miller, C. (2016, February 18). *Do Video Games Cause ADHD? Child Mind Institute.* https://childmind.org/article/do-video-games-cause-adhd/

Miller, G. (2021, July 22). *ADHD Parenting: 12 Tips to Tackle Common Challenges.* Psych Central. https://psychcentral.com/childhood-adhd/parenting-kids-with-adhd-tips-to-tackle-common-challenges#8.-Create-a-rewards-system-at-home

Morin, A. (2019). *The 8 Most Effective Ways to Discipline a Child With ADHD.* Verywell Family. https://www.verywellfamily.com/discipline-strategies-for-kids-with-adhd-1094941

Morin, A. (2021, October 25). *10 Fun Ways to Help Your Child Gain Better Impulse Control.* Verywell Family. https://www.verywellfamily.com/ways-to-teach-children-impulse-control-1095035

Morris-Rosendahl, D. J. (2020). Neurodevelopmental disorders—the history and future of a diagnostic concept. *Dialogues in Clinical Neuroscience, 22*(1), 65–72. https://doi.org/10.31887/dcns.2020.22.1/macrocq

NeuroHealth Associates. (2020, October 23). *The 9 Best Treatments for Children and Adults with ADHD.* NeuroHealth Associates. https://nhahealth.com/the-9-best-treatments-for-children-and-adults-with-adhd/

Newmark, S. (2019, February 6). *10 ADHD Supplements and Vitamins for Symptom Control.* ADDitude. https://www.additudemag.com/vitamins-minerals-adhd-treatment-plan/

NHS Choices. (2019). *Treatment - Attention deficit hyperactivity disorder (ADHD). NHS.* https://www.nhs.uk/conditions/attention-deficit-hyperactivity-disorder-adhd/treatment/

Nigg, J. (2020, August 27). *The ADHD-Anger Connection: New Insights into Emotional Dysregulation and Treatment Considerations*. ADDitude. https://www.additudemag.com/anger-issues-adhd-emotional-dysregulation/

Peasgood, T., Bhardwaj, A., Biggs, K., Brazier, J. E., Coghill, D., Cooper, C. L., Daley, D., De Silva, C., Harpin, V., Hodgkins, P., Nadkarni, A., Setyawan, J., & Sonuga-Barke, E. J. S. (2016). The impact of ADHD on the health and well-being of ADHD children and their siblings. *European Child & Adolescent Psychiatry*, 25(11), 1217–1231. https://doi.org/10.1007/s00787-016-0841-6

Porter, E. (2017, October 13). *Parenting Tips for ADHD: Do's and Don'ts*. Healthline; Healthline Media. https://www.healthline.com/health/adhd/parenting-tips#what-to-do

Professionals Who Diagnose and Treat ADHD. (n.d.). CHADD. https://chadd.org/about-adhd/professionals-who-diagnose-and-treat-adhd/

Ramnarace, C. (2016, January 14). *ADHD Discipline Techniques*. Everyday Health. https://www.everydayhealth.com/adhd/adhd-and-discipline.aspx

Raspolich, J. (n.d.). *Can ADHD Impact Your Memory?* Vista Pines Health. https://vistapineshealth.com/treatment/adhd/impact-memory/

Recognizing Early Signs of ADHD | Children's Community Pediatrics. (n.d.). Children's Community Pediatrics. Retrieved December 30, 2021, from https://www.childrenspeds.com/health-resources/social-emotional-well-being/recognizing-adhd

Regier, D. A., Kuhl, E. A., & Kupfer, D. J. (2013). The DSM-5: Classification and criteria changes. *World Psychiatry*, 12(2), 92–98. https://doi.org/10.1002/wps.20050

Rosen, P. (n.d.). *8 ways to help kids with ADHD cope with divorce*. Understood. Retrieved January 9, 2022, from https://www.understood.org/articles/en/8-ways-to-help-kids-with-adhd-cope-with-divorce

S, Newmark. (2016, February 4). *Can Psychotherapy Help Adult ADHD?* ADDitude. https://www.additudemag.com/adhd-psychotherapy/#:~:text=A%20lot%20of%20research%20has

Saline, S. (2018, August 6). *5 common mistakes parents make with their ADHD kids and how to fix them.* The Philadelphia Inquirer. https://www.inquirer.com/philly/health/kids-families/5-common-mistakes-parents-make-with-their-adhd-kids-and-how-to-fix-them-20180806.html

Storebø, O. J., Rasmussen, P. D., & Simonsen, E. (2013). Association Between Insecure Attachment and ADHD. *Journal of Attention Disorders,* 20(2), 187–196. https://doi.org/10.1177/1087054713501079

Substance Abuse and Mental Health Services Administration. (2016, June). *DSM-5 Child Mental Disorder Classification.* Nih.gov; Substance Abuse and Mental Health Services Administration (US). https://www.ncbi.nlm.nih.gov/books/NBK519712/

These 7 Herbs May Help Treat ADHD. (2021, July 29). Healthline. https://www.healthline.com/health/adhd/herbal-remedies#takeaway

Understood Team. (n.d.). *ADHD and anger.* Understood. https://www.understood.org/articles/en/adhd-and-anger-what-you-need-to-know

Wignall, N. (2021, July 25). *5 Rules for Setting Healthy Boundaries.* Nick Wignall. https://nickwignall.com/5-rules-for-setting-healthy-boundaries/

Made in the USA
Columbia, SC
10 January 2023

10035962R00096